AMERICA'S
NATIONAL PARKS

A Photographic Journey Through Nearly 400 National Treasures

2●16
National Park Service
CENTENNIAL

Eastern National
Serving the Visitors to America's
National Parks and Other Public Trusts

The images in this book were taken by National Park Service personnel, volunteers in the parks, cooperating association employees, and park visitors. The photographs were submitted in response to a nationwide request seeking views of every site in the National Park System. To date, there are more than 400 parks in the United States, American Samoa, Guam, Puerto Rico, and the Virgin Islands. One photograph of every park unit is included in this book.

The book is arranged in chronological order based on the date of the park's authorization or establishment, starting with Yellowstone National Park in 1872, up to the newest park, Waco Mammoth National Monument in 2015.

Special thanks to all National Park Service employees who submitted photographs and who helped in the production of this book. Thanks also to park volunteers and all who visit our national parks.

Published by Eastern National, copyright 2015
ISBN 978-1-59091-171-6

Eastern National
470 Maryland Drive
Fort Washington, PA 19034

Eastern National promotes the public's understanding and support of America's national parks
and other public trust partners by providing quality educational experiences, products, and services.

For more information about park-related publications and products, visit www.eParks.com

In 2016, the National Park Service will be 100 years old, and I will have served for 40 of those years. Starting as a seasonal ranger in 1976 on the National Mall when our nation celebrated its bicentennial, my career will be culminated with serving as the 18th director when the National Park Service celebrates its centennial. Over that course of four decades, I worked as ranger, biologist, or superintendent in eight different national parks, from the deserts of Guadalupe Mountains NP, to the snowy cascades of Crater Lake NP, to the wilds of Alaska at Wrangell-St. Elias NP. I also served for seven years as the regional director in the Pacific West, overseeing the solemn waters that cradle the USS *Arizona* at Pearl Harbor, the barbed wire around the Japanese American prison camp at Manzanar, and the stark beauty of Death Valley.

I am often asked by reporters and the public, "What is your favorite national park?" I laugh and reply that I love all my children. But it is true, I do love them all. I have special affection for those where I served, where my two kids were born, where my wife and I have had unparalleled experiences with nature and history, but each of the units of the national park system is unique and wonderful in their own terms. Comparing the hallways of Little Rock Central High School or the workshops of the Wright brothers with the Colorado River running through the Grand Canyon is an exercise in futility. Each one stands on its own, as testament to our history, our values, and our future.

Two things do bind them all; the first is that there are stewards of each, extraordinary people in ranger hats, educated and trained to be professionals at the highest standard of public service, whether it is to share with you a compelling story, to clean up after you leave, or to come find you if you are lost. They want you to come, experience, and deepen your understanding. The second attribute that binds all the national parks is conveyed in a 1970 Act of Congress, commonly known as the General Authorities Act. Congress said that though the parks are "distinct in character," they are "united…into one national park system as cumulative expressions of a single national heritage." These amazing parks await you, and this volume is an invitation to experience the places that remind us of what it means to be an American citizen.

— JONATHAN B. JARVIS

NATURE
HISTORY
CULTURE
CONNECTED

Yosemite. Yellowstone. The Statue of Liberty. Hot Springs. Canyon de Chelly. Devils Tower. Everglades. Shenandoah. Manzanar. Denali. Independence Hall. Chamizal. Appomattox. More than 400 special places—an extraordinary system of national parks that we, the American people, have fashioned for almost two hundred years.

Places, people, and events—where the compelling chapters in our shared heritage are retold and where landscapes provide tranquility, self-reflection, and exhilaration as new horizons and possibilities are made evident.

In 2016, our nation will celebrate the centennial of the National Park Service. Begun on August 25, 1916, through the prodigious efforts of Stephen T. Mather and Horace M. Albright, the first and second directors, respectively, the National Park Service now numbers more than 22,000 employees and 221,000 volunteers.

Today, the National Park Service provides a wide array of activities, services, and programs: from welcoming visitors, to interpreting natural, historical, and cultural sites. From monitoring climate change, to conducting state-of-the-art scientific, historical, and archeological research. From assisting with urban renewal adjacent to our urban parks, to offering "Living History" and environmental education programs. From working alongside our Volunteers-In-Parks, to cooperating with other nations in establishing World Heritage Sites. From partnerships with schools and universities, to working with neighboring communities and concessioners helping visitors enjoy their park experience.

The National Park Service is an incredible cadre of diverse people with different interests, expertise, languages, and backgrounds—all seeking to serve the citizens of the United States and the peoples of the world so that the national parks may be enjoyed and preserved unimpaired for future generations.

In our rootless, restless society, we need a place to discover who we are; a special place that is as constant as love, as transcendent and powerful as the change of seasons, as joyous as the laughter of a child, as exhilarating and re-creating as freedom itself. That special place is found in our national parks—a unique creation that is admired and emulated around the world.

At Yellowstone, Everglades, Olympic, Isle Royale, Cape Hatteras, and Padre Island, we have saved vignettes of our diverse landscapes and seascapes. At Yosemite, Grand Canyon, Katmai, Great Sand Dunes, and Hawai`i Volcanoes, we stand in awe of the geological forces that have carved and shaped our land. At Mesa Verde, Gila Cliff Dwellings, Canyon de Chelly, Chaco Culture, and other shrines of antiquity, we have preserved the remnants of indigenous cultures.

From first blood at Bunker Hill, through the snows of Valley Forge, onto the battlefields of Cowpens and Kings Mountain, and into the trenches of Yorktown, we commemorate the sacrifice, the courage, and the valor of those who laid the foundations of our freedom.

At Independence National Historical Park, Hamilton Grange, and the historic district of Washington, D.C., we preserve the monuments and remember the legacy of those who wrote our Constitution and chartered our democracy.

At Gettysburg, Vicksburg, Fredericksburg, Manassas, Appomattox, and scores of other battlefields, we stand in silent reverence amidst the reminders of the purging fires of war that forged anew the bonds of union.

At Fort Raleigh where English settlement was first attempted, at Jamestown where it first succeeded; at Cabrillo, Castillo de San Marcos, Castle Clinton, Ellis Island, and the Statue of Liberty, we remember those who came to this land. And at Cumberland Gap, Whitman Mission, and dozens of other landmarks along the trails to the American West, we can walk where our ancestors walked. We can see where they encountered the many indigenous peoples and their nations whose sovereign life ways still form important traditions today.

At Saugus Iron Works, Thomas Edison's laboratory, Golden Spike, and the Wright Brothers memorial, we honor the pioneers whose creative genius undergirded our industrial and economic might. At memorials to women's rights, Carl Sandburg, Frederick Douglass, Eleanor Roosevelt, Martin Luther King, Jr., Roger Williams, Mary McLeod Bethune, and César E. Chávez, we lift up the hope that our love of justice, equality, and liberty may be as matchless as our industrial and economic strength.

Theodore Roosevelt NP

At Ford's Theatre, Wolf Trap, and New Orleans Jazz, we celebrate the passion, pathos, and ingenuity of the human spirit.

Throughout the centuries, places set aside for special purposes, such as parks, have evolved and expanded—from Nebuchadnezzar's Hanging Gardens of Babylon to New York City's Central Park, from regional forest preserves to Washington, D.C.'s National Mall of monuments and museums, from Yellowstone National Park to amusement parks, from backyards to international biosphere reserves— the park idea has continued to grow and change.

Acadia NP

Since March 1, 1872, when Yellowstone was established as the world's first "national" park, more than 180 nations have set aside similar parks and preserves. Today, parks—natural, historical, cultural, recreational, and sacred—around the world are owned and managed by governments (federal, state, regional, or municipal), indigenous peoples, charitable organizations, private enterprise, or partnerships as well as those managed by communities through traditional and customary means.

This international and interrelated network of parks and protected areas serves as:

- *Expressions of local, regional, tribal, and national self-understanding and the values of a people.*
- *The "miner's canary," giving forewarning of the changes in the natural and human condition.*
- *Bridges for mutual understanding among the world's diverse communities.*

Significantly, the world's parks and protected areas share a common "language" that gives expression to the diversity of identity and interest among the peoples of the world and, also, their shared heritage in the world community.

These parks and protected sites help us to be in touch with the superlative beauty and grandeur of creation as well as to contemplate the interrelatedness of life and the forces that shape and sustain our world. They are places where we can discover and appreciate the cultures and communities, the women, men, and children who have shaped our society—their courage and compassion, their inventiveness and perseverance, their strengths and weaknesses, their failings, faults, and follies as well as their signal achievements against the odds.

The national parks have set aside the superb and sublime vistas of our geography; they have sought to preserve the inspiriting visions and accomplishments of our nation as well as the "untold stories" and difficult chapters of our society. Indeed, these special places are more than physical resources; they are the delicate strands of nature and culture that bond the generations.

Yet, in the early years of the 21st century, the issues that face (and jeopardize) the world's parks and protected areas are enormous and urgent. Often they exceed the boundaries of the parks and are beyond the conventional scope of park management.

The challenge of a threatened biosphere, growing economic disparity and poverty, globalization and ethnic strife, terrorism and war, the destruction of cultural landscapes and historic sites, the disappearance of flora and fauna, the pandemics of human illness and hunger, political upheaval, widespread corruption, and unprecedented immigration make vivid the urgency posed to conscience. Amid these sea changes, are parks and protected areas relevant to the human experience and the quality of life?

As Freeman Tilden, the noted park interpreter, wrote, the national parks are about the question, "Who am I?" Today, the "web of life"—human and natural—while strong and vibrant, also is strained and in disrepair. As a teacher wrote some years ago: "There is one web of life. You are a part of it. The web is in trouble—and you can do something about it." Can the park experience be re-creative, personally and collectively for humankind?

Indeed, this is a "kairos" moment in history and the park movement—kairos being the ancient Greek term for a special moment that is ripe for action. Since George Catlin first proposed the national park idea in 1832, the great moral and ethical issues have been the raison d'être of the park movement.

Yes, the national parks—those natural, historical, recreational and cultural landmarks—are where we can be "in touch" with the natural rhythms of the Earth and its delicate balances—and where we can discover the intricate fabric of civilization and the beauty of its multifaceted peoples. In a very real way, the national parks can help us understand who we are and who we can be—and how we can make a creative difference in our communities and the world in which we live.

If parks are to be renewing and relevant, if parks are to maintain their integrity, we must come to terms with the most critical issues facing our society and the great ideas which form our common life: liberty, justice, and equality; truth, goodness, and beauty. It is with such a new and expanded park idea as catalyst and conscience that the parks will be preserved for the generations and that our park experiences can help us create a quality of life for all humankind.

THE AUTHORS

George B. Hartzog, Jr. *was the seventh director of the National Park Service (1964-1973). He was instrumental in the passage of the Land and Water Conservation Fund, the National Historic Preservation Act, the Wilderness Act, and the National Wild and Scenic Rivers Act.*

George B. Hartzog, III *is a retired United Methodist minister and served as president of the Navajo Methodist Mission School. He is a former national park ranger and a life member of the Association of National Park Rangers, the Employee and Alumni Association, and the George Wright Society.*

LITTLE BIGHORN BATTLEFIELD NM
Montana, 1886

Lt. Col. George Custer's 263 cavalrymen faced several thousand Northern Plains tribesmen in 1876 at this site. Though it was a great victory for the Indians, it was the beginning of the end for their way of life.

YELLOWSTONE NP
Wyoming, Montana, Idaho, 1872

Yellowstone, the world's first national park, is home to Old Faithful, more than 10,000 thermal features, and a stunning array of wildlife.

CHICKAMAUGA AND CHATTANOOGA NMP
Georgia, Tennessee, 1890

The first national military park preserves Civil War battlefields where a Confederate victory in September 1863 was followed by Union victories two months later.

CASA GRANDE RUINS NM
Arizona, 1889

Casa Grande, a three- to four-story adobe structure, was built by the Hohokam who farmed in the Gila Valley in the early 1200s. It was abandoned by the mid-1400s.

SEQUOIA NP
California, 1890

This park in the High Sierra is home to giant sequoia trees—the world's largest living things—and is the location of Mount Whitney, the highest mountain in the United States outside of Alaska.

KINGS CANYON NP
California, 1890

Originally established as General Grant NP, Kings Canyon encompasses a portion of the High Sierra and two enormous canyons of the Kings River.

ANTIETAM NB
Maryland, 1890

Confederate Gen. Robert E. Lee's first attempt to invade the North ended in a Confederate retreat, giving President Lincoln the occasion to propose the Emancipation Proclamation.

ROCK CREEK PARK
Washington, D.C., 1890

Rock Creek, running north to south and emptying into the Potomac River, is a refuge of wilderness within the Nation's Capital. It is one of the largest natural urban parks in the United States.

YOSEMITE NP
California, 1890

Yosemite Valley was first protected by legislation signed by President Lincoln in 1864. Today, it preserves alpine meadows, forests, valleys, wildlife, and the highest waterfall in the United States.

SHILOH NMP
Tennessee, Mississippi, 1894

The Civil War battle fought here in 1862 was part of the struggle to control railroads in middle Tennessee and northern Mississippi. A separate unit interprets the Battle of Corinth, Mississippi.

VICKSBURG NMP
Mississippi, 1899

The Civil War siege of Vicksburg that ended in a Union victory, July 4, 1863, gave Union forces control of the entire Mississippi River, effectively splitting the Confederacy in two.

GETTYSBURG NMP
Pennsylvania, 1895

Gen. Robert E. Lee's second invasion of the North ended in a Union victory on July 3, 1863. Lee made no more attempts to carry the war into the North. A national cemetery adjoins the park.

CHICKASAW NRA
Oklahoma, 1902

The springs, lakes, campsites, and hiking trails
within the forested hills honor the original
inhabitants of this land, the Chickasaws.

MOUNT RAINIER NP
Washington, 1899

The landscape surrounding this ancient
volcano is home to forests, meadows, temperate
rain forests, and wildlife. Some parts of the
park receive nearly 54 feet of snow each year.

CRATER LAKE NP
Oregon, 1902

Approximately 7,700 years ago, a volcano erupted, blowing off its top and creating a lake inside the remains that is almost 2,000 feet deep, making it the deepest lake in the United States.

WIND CAVE NP
South Dakota, 1903

These prairies and forests are where east meets west in a richness of wildlife and vegetation. The cave that lies beneath is an entirely different world with elaborate boxwork and calcite crystal formations.

DEVILS TOWER NM
Wyoming, 1906

An astounding geologic feature that protrudes out of the rolling prairie surrounding the Black Hills, this site is considered sacred to the Lakota and other tribes. It was the first national monument in the United States.

EL MORRO NM
New Mexico, 1906

Early travelers carved signatures, dates, and messages into the soft sandstone. The monument includes pre-Columbian petroglyphs and the remains of Pueblo Indian dwellings.

MESA VERDE NP
Colorado, 1906

Mesa Verde offers a spectacular look into the lives of the Ancestral Puebloan people who made it their home from 600 to 1300. Today, the park protects nearly 5,000 known archeological sites, including 600 cliff dwellings.

MONTEZUMA CASTLE NM
Arizona, 1906

This five-story structure with 20 rooms was built between the 1100s and 1200s and is one of the best-preserved cliff dwellings in North America.

PETRIFIED FOREST NP
Arizona, 1906

At least nine different species of trees have been identified in the petrified remains of ancient forest. The park is rich in other fossils—notably plants and reptiles.

CHACO CULTURE NHP
New Mexico, 1907

Hundreds of years ago, this area was the home of a thriving community of Ancestral Puebloan people. Their elaborate structures remain to illustrate their way of life.

JEAN LAFITTE NHP & PRES
Louisiana, 1907

This park contains sites that interpret the Acadian past of southern Louisiana as well as Chalmette Battlefield, the site of the 1815 Battle of New Orleans.

GILA CLIFF DWELLINGS NM

New Mexico, 1907

This remote canyon contains five cliff dwellings built by
Mogollon people, the only such site in the United States.
It was inhabited from about 1280 to the early 1300s.

TONTO NM
Arizona, 1907

Two cliff dwellings, colorful pottery, woven cotton cloth, and other artifacts tell a story of people living and using resources from the northern Sonoran Desert from 1250 to 1450.

LASSEN VOLCANIC NP
California, 1907

Lassen Volcano erupted several times between 1914 and 1921. This is the southernmost volcano in the Cascade Range that extends into British Columbia. The site features boiling springs and sulfurous vents.

JEWEL CAVE NM
South Dakota, 1908

Limestone caverns consisting of a series of chambers can be found here. More than 177 miles of passageways have been mapped, and the cave has even more to explore.

MUIR WOODS NM
California, 1908

John Muir, for whom the park was named, said that it was "the best tree-lovers monument that could possibly be found in all the forests of the world." It contains many towering redwood trees.

PINNACLES NP
California, 1908

Come seek out the California condor in the High Peaks, explore the rare chaparral vegetation and carpets of wildflowers, or hike among the breathtaking spires and rock formations.

NATURAL BRIDGES NM
Utah, 1908

Three natural bridges carved out of sandstone, including the second and third largest in the world, are protected here. Ancestral Puebloan rock art and the remains of ancient structures are also present.

TUMACÁCORI NHP
Arizona, 1908

This Spanish Catholic mission stands near the site first visited by a Jesuit priest in 1691. The site includes a partially restored Franciscan church that is still used for special events.

NAVAJO NM
Arizona, 1909

Three ancient cliff-dwelling ruins are preserved here. The prehistoric Puebloan ancestors built their villages within the natural sandstone alcoves of the canyons between 1250 to 1300.

OLYMPIC NP
Washington, 1909

This park features 73 miles of Pacific coastline, snowcapped mountains, Roosevelt elk, and a large temperate rain forest.

OREGON CAVES
NM & PRES
Oregon, 1909

Nestled deep inside mountains, the caves formed as rainwater from the ancient forest above dissolved the surrounding marble and created a special cave system.

SITKA NHP
Alaska, 1910

The park preserves the remains of Russian efforts to establish a colony in North America and to exploit the rich fur resources of Alaska. Tlingit and Haida totem poles stand along the park's scenic coastal trail.

ZION NP
Utah, 1909

Deep, narrow canyons, high mesas, and a variety of habitats based on elevation provide a bountiful variety of plant and animal life. Massive sandstone cliffs of cream, pink, and red soar into a brilliant blue sky.

GLACIER NP
Montana, 1910

Sitting on the Continental Divide, the park preserves many glaciers, dense forest, lakes fed by glacial meltwater, and a rich collection of wildlife.

SALINAS PUEBLO MISSIONS NM
New Mexico, 1909

The mission's three sites interpret a history entrenched with cultural borrowing, conflict, and struggles. The now-abandoned sites stand as reminders of the Spanish and Pueblo People's early encounters.

BIG HOLE NB
Montana, 1910

The site commemorates the battle between the Nez Perce Indians and U.S. Infantry forces in August 1877. Ninety Nez Perce men, women, and children, and 31 soldiers and volunteers lost their lives.

RAINBOW BRIDGE NM
Utah, 1910

This salmon-pink sandstone formation is the world's largest natural bridge. It rises 290 feet above the floor of Bridge Canyon. Neighboring American Indian tribes considered Rainbow Bridge a sacred site.

LINCOLN MEMORIAL
Washington, D.C., 1911

The memorial sits on the banks of the Potomac River, facing the U.S. Capitol. The 19-foot-high marble statue of Abraham Lincoln is an enduring symbol of unity, strength, and wisdom. The memorial was dedicated in 1922.

COLORADO NM
Colorado, 1911

In western Colorado's sandstone country, the cliffs, monoliths, arches, and remains of Indian cultures can be found. You may also see bighorn sheep and soaring eagles.

DEVILS POSTPILE NM
California, 1911

Flowing basalt cooled and formed columns that resemble a giant pipe organ. The longest columns are 60 feet high. The park protects the 101-foot-high Rainbow Falls and pristine mountain scenery.

CABRILLO NM
California, 1913

In 1542, Juan Rodriguez Cabrillo was the first European to set foot on what is now the West Coast of the United States. This park honors his explorations.

ROCKY MOUNTAIN NP
Colorado, 1915

A number of peaks above 14,000 feet, diverse wildlife, miles of hiking trails, and the headwaters of the Colorado River are found within the park's 415 square miles.

DINOSAUR NM
Colorado, Utah, 1915

The park is known for its dinosaur quarry, among the best in the world. The canyon and landscapes created by the Green and Yampa rivers are ideal for rafting and hiking.

31

ACADIA NP
Maine, 1916

The rising sun first touches Cadillac Mountain in Acadia, highlighting carriage roads for biking and hiking, as well as miles of rocky and sandy beaches for access to the Atlantic Ocean.

CAPULIN VOLCANO NM
New Mexico, 1916

This symmetrical cinder cone is an example of a geologically recent, inactive volcano. The dramatic landscape was created by forces that reshaped the terrain.

ABRAHAM LINCOLN BIRTHPLACE NHP
Kentucky, 1916

A cabin similar to that in which Abraham Lincoln was born is located in the Memorial Building. Lincoln and his family lived here until they moved to Indiana when he was seven.

WALNUT CANYON NM
Arizona, 1915

Among the remarkable geological cliff formations of the canyon, the shapes of the former homes of ancient inhabitants are evident. Walk in the steps of those who came before us.

HALEAKALĀ NP
Hawaii, 1916

The highest point of the park is above 10,000 feet, and the lowest is at sea level. Such an elevation difference results in a widely varied array of plant and animal life.

BANDELIER NM
New Mexico, 1916

Remains of Indian dwellings can be found on the mesa tops and in the canyon walls, all dating from the 13th century.

35

DENALI NP & PRES
Alaska, 1917

At 20,320 feet, Mount McKinley is the highest mountain in North America. The surrounding park is home to caribou, Dall sheep, moose, grizzlies, and wolves, as well as a splendid subarctic landscape.

HAWAI'I VOLCANOES NP
Hawaii, 1916

Few parks have volcanoes that erupt regularly. This one does. During a volcanic eruption, we are reminded that our planet is an ever-changing environment. The park is an international biosphere reserve and a world heritage site.

KENNESAW MOUNTAIN NBP
Georgia, 1917

During the Civil War, Gen. William T. Sherman's advance on Atlanta was temporarily halted here by a Confederate victory in June 1864.

GUILFORD COURTHOUSE NMP
North Carolina, 1917

Though the British Army won the battle of Guilford Courthouse in 1781, its massive losses contributed to their eventual surrender at Yorktown, Va., seven months later.

KATMAI NP & PRES
Alaska, 1918

In over four million acres, wildlife roam in abundance, the rivers are filled with salmon, and some thermal features remain from the 1912 volcano eruption.

SCOTTS BLUFF NM
Nebraska, 1919

Pioneers moving westward along the Platte River Valley looked for landmarks in the rolling prairies to let them know they were making progress; Scotts Bluff was one such landmark.

GRAND CANYON NP
Arizona, 1919

Peering into the Grand Canyon, more than a mile deep at points, gives special meaning to the word "breathtaking." The Colorado River flows for 277 miles through this natural wonder of geologic color and erosional forms.

HOT SPRINGS NP
Arkansas, 1921

Established in 1832, Hot Springs was the first federal reservation and became a national park in 1921. The park includes eight historically significant bathhouses, hiking trails, and scenic drives.

YUCCA HOUSE NM
Colorado, 1919

This is one of the largest archeological sites in southwest Colorado, and the extent of the remains at Yucca House is not yet completely known. Archeological work will reveal the nature of the site.

GREAT BASIN NP
Nevada, 1922

Arches, natural tunnels, an ancient bristlecone pine forest, beautiful Lehman Caves, and the remains of an icefield on 13,000-foot Wheeler Peak, are some of the features of Great Basin.

TIMPANOGOS CAVE NM
Utah, 1922

Three caves in a mountainside, accessible by a steep trail, contain formations that grow in all directions, apparently disregarding gravity.

AZTEC RUINS NM
New Mexico, 1923

Ancestral Puebloan peoples built the structures located here from the 1100s. You can explore a 900-year-old Great House of over 400 masonry rooms.

HOVENWEEP NM
Utah, Colorado, 1923

Ancestral Puebloan towers, structures, and cliff dwellings scattered along canyon rims give an impression of life in this sometimes harsh, semiarid landscape.

PIPE SPRING NM
Arizona, 1923

American Indians, Mormon pioneers, and many others have depended on the water found at Pipe Spring. Learn about pioneer and Kaibab Paiute life by exploring the historic fort and garden.

HOPEWELL CULTURE NHP
Ohio, 1923

Burial mounds and large geometric earthworks provide insight into the life of the Hopewell people who lived here from 200 BCE to 500.

43

This magical area along the edge of high-plateau country contains exotic landforms, colorful pinnacles, walls, and spires. Seasonal displays of wildflowers add to the enchantment.

CRATERS OF THE MOON NM & PRES
Idaho, 1924

Lava flows more than 2,000 years old have created a landscape that many view as otherworldly. Within the lava flows are scattered islands of cinder cones and sagebrush.

CARLSBAD CAVERNS NP
New Mexico, 1923

The rooms within the cave are enormous; the Big Room is about eight acres in size. Bats that live in the caverns usually emerge en masse at sunset.

CHIRICAHUA NM
Arizona, 1924

The park is famous for unusual rock formations created millions of years ago by volcanic activity. A cattle ranch on the site has been restored.

STATUE OF LIBERTY NM
New York, 1924

The statue was a gift from the people of France to the people of the United States to commemorate their alliance during the American Revolution. The monument has become a universal icon of freedom.

CASTILLO DE SAN MARCOS NM
Florida, 1924

The Castillo is located in Saint Augustine, the oldest permanent European settlement in the United States. The fort dates from 1672.

FORT MATANZAS NM
Florida, 1924

This Spanish watchtower was built from 1740 to 1742, to guard against a possible British, or other enemy, attack on Saint Augustine.

FORT PULASKI NM
Georgia, 1924

The massive brick fortress with walls up to 11 feet thick took 18 years to build. During the Civil War, newly developed rifled cannon pierced the fort in only 30 hours of bombardment.

MOUNT RUSHMORE N MEM
South Dakota, 1925

The heads of four great American presidents—George Washington, Thomas Jefferson, Theodore Roosevelt, and Abraham Lincoln—were carved into the face of a granite mountain in South Dakota's Black Hills.

FORT McHENRY NM & HS
Maryland, 1925

Francis Scott Key witnessed the bombardment of the fort during the War of 1812. The poem that he wrote based upon his observations—*The Star-Spangled Banner*—is now the U.S. national anthem.

GLACIER BAY NP & PRES
Alaska, 1925

Tidewater glaciers calving into the ocean, seals, eagles, mountains, whales, and amazing sea and wildlife make this park an incredible destination.

WUPATKI NM
Arizona, 1924

Located between the Painted Desert and ponderosa highlands, Wupatki is a landscape where ancient pueblos dot red rock outcroppings across miles of prairie.

SHENANDOAH NP
Virginia, 1926

Cascading waterfalls, spectacular vistas, and quiet wooded hollows can be discovered within these 200,000 acres of protected lands. Scenic Skyline Drive traverses the mountains.

LAVA BEDS NM
California, 1925

More than 700 caves, Native American rock art sites, historic battlefields and campsites, and a high-desert wilderness are here in this rugged landscape.

ARLINGTON HOUSE, THE ROBERT E. LEE MEMORIAL
Virginia, 1925

The house was built by George Washington Parke Custis, the step-grandson of George Washington. His daughter married Robert E. Lee. Today, the family estate is the site of Arlington Cemetery.

MAMMOTH CAVE NP
Kentucky, 1926

More than 400 miles of passageways have been
mapped, making this one of the world's most
extensive cave systems. The park also preserves
a part of the Green River Valley and hilly
country of south central Kentucky.

MOORES CREEK NB
North Carolina, 1926

During this Revolutionary War battle, loyalists
encountered nearly 1,000 patriots with cannons
and muskets. This dramatic victory for the patriots
ended British rule in the colony forever.

STONES RIVER NB
Tennessee, 1927

Fighting took place in bitter winter weather during the Civil War as both sides struggled to control rail lines in middle Tennessee. Three days of fighting ended with Union forces controlling the field.

PETERSBURG NB
Virginia, 1926

Petersburg was the key to the important Confederate stronghold of Richmond during the Civil War. A 10-month siege eventually resulted in Union success and opened the road to Richmond.

FREDERICKSBURG AND SPOTSYLVANIA COUNTY BATTLEFIELDS MEMORIAL NMP
Virginia, 1927

This park consists of four major Civil War battlefields: Fredericksburg, Chancellorsville, Wilderness, and Spotsylvania Court House. The outcomes of each battle had important consequences for both sides.

TUPELO NB
Mississippi, 1929

In July 1864, Civil War troops engaged in a fierce fight in Tupelo. The Union achieved its goal: keeping Confederates from cutting the Union's crucial railroad supply line.

BRICES CROSS ROADS NBS
Mississippi, 1929

This Civil War battle was fought to protect Union supply lines, and though the Confederates were outnumbered, they prevailed and drove the Union troops from the field.

WRIGHT BROTHERS N MEM
North Carolina, 1927

Wind, sand, and a dream of flight brought Wilbur and Orville Wright to the Outer Banks, where, after four years of experimentation, they achieved the first successful airplane flight on December 17, 1903.

FORT DONELSON NB
Tennessee, 1928

The Union victories here in February 1862 thrilled the North and shocked the South. Gen. Ulysses S. Grant captured three forts and opened two rivers, making him a national figure.

With extraordinary wildlife, pristine lakes,
and miles of trails through alpine terrain, the
Teton Range stands as a monument to the
people who fought to protect it.

COWPENS NB
South Carolina, 1929

In 1781, Brig. Gen. Daniel Morgan won a notable victory over British forces in this South Carolina pasture, helping to ensure the future of the American cause during the Revolutionary War.

GEORGE WASHINGTON BIRTHPLACE NM
Virginia, 1930

George Washington, preeminent leader of the American Revolutionary War and first U.S. president, was born in 1732 at his father's plantation on Popes Creek in Westmoreland County, Virginia.

SUNSET CRATER VOLCANO NM
Arizona, 1930

Roughly 900 years ago, the eruption of this volcano reshaped the landscape around it. Today, dramatic geological features coexist with twisted ponderosa pines.

ARCHES NP
Utah, 1929

A landscape of contrasting colors, landforms, and textures, this red rock wonderland has over 2,000 natural stone arches, hundreds of soaring pinnacles, massive fins, and giant balanced rocks.

COLONIAL NHP
Virginia, 1930

Jamestown commemorates the first permanent English settlement in North America in 1607, and Yorktown is where the British were defeated in the last major battle of the American Revolutionary War in 1781. The 23-mile-long Colonial Parkway connects the two sites.

GEORGE WASHINGTON MEMORIAL PARKWAY
Washington, D.C., Maryland, Virginia, 1930

The parkway is a memorial to America's first president, George Washington. It connects Mount Vernon, Alexandria, Washington, D.C., and the Great Falls of the Potomac.

CANYON DE CHELLY NM
Arizona, 1931

For almost 5,000 years, people have lived in these canyons. Today, Navajo families continue to make their homes, raise livestock, and farm the lands in the canyon.

APPOMATTOX COURT HOUSE NHP
Virginia, 1930

On April 9, 1865, the surrender of the Confederate Army of Northern Virginia took place in this small village and signaled the end of the Civil War. The tattered nation was once again intact.

FORT NECESSITY NB
Pennsylvania, 1931

The British, French, and American Indians fought at Fort Necessity, the opening action of the French and Indian War, which set the stage for the American Revolution.

ISLE ROYALE NP
Michigan, 1931

Surrounded by Lake Superior, this park is the largest wilderness area in Michigan and a place of unparalleled solitude and stunning scenic beauty.

GREAT SAND DUNES NP & PRES
Colorado, 1932

The tallest dunes in North America are also one of the most fragile and complex dune systems in the world. Elevations range from 8,000 to over 13,000 feet.

KINGS MOUNTAIN NMP
South Carolina, 1931

This site commemorates a turning point of the Revolutionary War where a patriot victory on October 7, 1780, changed the course of the war.

WHITE SANDS NM
New Mexico, 1933

White Sands National Monument protects part of the world's largest gypsum dune field, covering 275 square miles. The plants and animals here have adapted to extreme conditions.

THEODORE ROOSEVELT ISLAND
Washington, D.C., 1932

This wooded island sanctuary in the Potomac River was designed as a tribute to the conservation-minded 26th president of the United States.

BLACK CANYON OF THE GUNNISON NP
Colorado, 1933

Over the course of two million years, the Gunnison River joined the forces of nature to chisel this vertical wilderness of rock, water, and sky.

MORRISTOWN NHP
New Jersey, 1933

Troops of the Continental Army under Gen. George Washington survived the worst winter of the 18th century here during the 1779-1780 winter encampment.

SAGUARO NP
Arizona, 1933

Home to the nation's largest cacti, this desert park also marks the place where prehistoric Hohokam, homesteaders, and ranchers hunted, planted crops, tended livestock, and raised families.

DEATH VALLEY NP
California, 1933

In this below-sea-level basin, steady drought and record summer heat make Death Valley a land of extremes, where the temperature can exceed 120 degrees and winter snow can blanket towering peaks.

NATIONAL CAPITAL PARKS
Washington, D.C., 1933

The park system of the nation's capital comprises parks, parkways, and reservations in the District of Columbia, encompassing properties such as President's Park and the Battleground National Cemetery.

WASHINGTON MONUMENT
Washington, D.C., 1933

Built to honor our first president, this 555-foot marble obelisk towers over Washington, D.C., offering views of the District of Columbia, Maryland, and Virginia. The monument was dedicated in 1885.

NATIONAL MALL
Washington, D.C., 1933

The National Mall symbolizes our nation and its democratic values that inspire the world. The landscaped park extends from the foot of the Capitol to the Washington Monument.

WHITE HOUSE
Washington, D.C., 1933

One of the most recognizable buildings in Washington, D.C., the White House has been the residence and office of U.S. presidents since November 1800.

CEDAR BREAKS NM
Utah, 1933

Multicolored rock formations fill this half-mile-deep geologic amphitheater, creating a landscape that features spectacular views. Bristlecone pines and meadows of wildflowers enhance this rich, subalpine forest.

OCMULGEE NM
Georgia, 1934

Traces of 12,000 years of Southeastern culture from Ice Age Indians to the historic Creek Confederacy are preserved here. Mississippian temple mounds survive to this day.

EVERGLADES NP
Florida, 1934

Everglades National Park spans 1.5 million acres and protects the habitat for rare and endangered species including manatee, American crocodile, and Florida panther.

BIG BEND NP
Texas, 1935

Scenic vistas, diverse wildlife, historic sites, and border culture are among the features here where mountains contrast with desert within the great bend of the Rio Grande.

MONOCACY NB
Maryland, 1934

On July 9, 1864, Union troops at Monocacy Junction delayed Confederate forces for a day, long enough that Washington, D.C., defenses could be strengthened around the capital city.

GREAT SMOKY MOUNTAINS NP
Tennessee, North Carolina, 1934

Renowned for its diversity of plant and animal life, the beauty of its mountains, and the remnants of Southern Appalachian culture, this is one of America's most visited national parks.

THOMAS JEFFERSON MEMORIAL
Washington, D.C., 1934

Inside the circular colonnade, a 19-foot-tall statue of Thomas Jefferson stands holding the Declaration of Independence, a tribute to this founding father, revolutionary, and 3rd U.S. president. The memorial was dedicated in 1943.

ANDREW JOHNSON NHS
Tennessee, 1935

Visit the early home, tailor shop, homestead, and burial ground of the 17th president, who endured the Civil War and the struggles of Reconstruction.

BLUE RIDGE PARKWAY
North Carolina, Virginia, 1935

Protecting a diversity of plants and animals, the parkway meanders for 469 miles, revealing stunning long-range vistas of the rugged mountains and pastoral landscapes of the Appalachian Highlands.

FORT STANWIX NM
New York, 1935

Fort Stanwix was significant through the French and Indian War, the American Revolution, and as a gathering place for treaty signings with American Indians.

JEFFERSON NATIONAL EXPANSION MEMORIAL
Missouri, 1935

The memorial consists of the 630-foot Gateway Arch and St. Louis's Old Courthouse, site of the Dred Scott decision, which hastened the start of the Civil War.

PERRY'S VICTORY AND INTERNATIONAL PEACE MEMORIAL
Ohio, 1936

The memorial is a tribute to those who fought in the Battle of Lake Erie during the War of 1812 and to international peace by arbitration and disarmament.

HOMESTEAD NM OF AMERICA
Nebraska, 1936

The Homestead Act of 1862 changed the young nation with its offer of free land. The 160-acre claims offered not only new land but also new life.

FORT FREDERICA NM
Georgia, 1936

Gen. James E. Oglethorpe built this British town and fort in 1736-1748 during the Anglo-Spanish struggle for control of what is now the southeastern United States.

WHITMAN MISSION NHS
Washington, 1936

The mission was an important way station on the Oregon Trail. Cultural differences and a measles epidemic led the Cayuse Indians to violence and the death of the missionaries Marcus and Narcissa Whitman.

RICHMOND NBP
Virginia, 1936

The park commemorates numerous major Civil War battles around Richmond, including Gaines' Mill where 15,000 soldiers were killed, wounded, missing, or captured in one day.

CATOCTIN MOUNTAIN PARK
Maryland, 1936

This mountain park, part of the forested ridge that forms the eastern rampart of the Appalachian Mountains in Maryland, features sparkling streams and panoramic vistas.

PRINCE WILLIAM FOREST PARK
Virginia, 1936

At over 15,000 acres, Prince William Forest Park protects the largest example of eastern Piedmont forest in the National Park System.

JOSHUA TREE NP
California, 1936

This desert region features a representative stand of Joshua trees and a great variety of plants and animals coexisting in a vast wilderness.

CAPITOL REEF NP
Utah, 1937

A hidden treasure filled with cliffs, canyons, domes, and bridges in the Waterpocket Fold—a geologic wrinkle on the earth extending almost 100 miles.

ORGAN PIPE CACTUS NM
Arizona, 1937

Sonoran Desert plants and animals found nowhere else in the United States are protected here, as are signs of human use dating back to the 1500s.

CAPE HATTERAS NS
North Carolina, 1937

Ocean waves, a starry night sky, the calm of the salt marshes, waterfowl, and historic points of interest are all part of this first national seashore.

PIPESTONE NM
Minnesota, 1937

Winnewissa Falls is one of the beautiful features of this monument, which is also home to pipestone quarries that are a sacred site for many American Indians.

CHANNEL ISLANDS NP
California, 1938

Encompassing five islands and their ocean environment, the park is home to nesting sea birds, sea lion rookeries, and unique plants.

SARATOGA NHP
New York, 1938

The Battle of Saratoga in 1777 was a major American victory that assured international recognition and aid and helped secure the independence of the United States.

NATCHEZ TRACE PARKWAY
Mississippi, Alabama, Tennessee, 1938

From American Indian mounds and "Kaintucks" to historic stands and the Civil War, the Natchez Trace Parkway takes you on a 444-mile journey through "the Old Trace."

SALEM MARITIME NHS
Massachusetts, 1938

The historic buildings, wharves, and reconstructed tall ship here tell the stories of the sailors, Revolutionary War privateers, and merchants who brought the riches of the world to America.

FORT LARAMIE NHS
Wyoming, 1938

Established as a private fur trading post on the eastern Wyoming prairie in 1834, Fort Laramie evolved into the largest military post on the Northern Plains.

CHESAPEAKE AND OHIO CANAL NHP
Maryland, Washington, D.C.,
West Virginia, 1938

Built between 1828 and 1850, this 184.5-mile canal
was a lifeline for communities along the Potomac
River as coal, lumber, and agricultural products
were transported down the waterway to market.

BADLANDS NP
South Dakota, 1939

First called "mako sica" or "land bad"
by the Lakota, this place is an expanse of
mixed-grass prairie where bison,
bighorn sheep, and prairie dogs live.

TUZIGOOT NM
Arizona, 1939

Tuzigoot, an Apache word that means "crooked water," contains the ruins of a large Indian pueblo that flourished in the Verde Valley between 1100 and 1450.

HOPEWELL FURNACE NHS
Pennsylvania, 1938

One of the finest examples of a rural American iron plantation of the 1800s, Hopewell Furnace was founded in 1771 by Mark Bird, the first ironmaster.

FEDERAL HALL N MEM
New York, 1939

Located on Wall Street, this site is where our first president took the oath of office. It was home to the first Congress, Supreme Court, and Executive Branch offices.

MANASSAS NBP
Virginia, 1940

The First and Second Battles of Manassas were fought here July 21, 1861, and August 28-30, 1862. This is where Gen. Thomas J. Jackson acquired his nickname "Stonewall."

VANDERBILT MANSION NHS
New York, 1940

This palatial mansion provides a glimpse of estate life in the late 19th century and the world of the American millionaire during the Gilded Age.

CUMBERLAND GAP NHP
Kentucky, Virginia, Tennessee, 1940

Cumberland Gap was a main artery for settlers traveling west of the Appalachians following their dreams of prosperity. It was also an important military objective in the Civil War.

FORT WASHINGTON PARK
Maryland, 1940

Fort Washington has stood as silent sentry defending the Nation's Capital for over 200 years. It is one of the few remaining seacoast forts.

GEORGE WASHINGTON CARVER NM
Missouri, 1943

Nature and nurture influenced the young Carver on his quest for education to becoming a renowned agricultural scientist, educator, and humanitarian.

HOME OF FRANKLIN D. ROOSEVELT NHS
New York, 1944

FDR's Springwood, the estate that he loved, was the place he considered home. Visit to learn about the only U.S. president elected to four terms.

FORT RALEIGH NHS
North Carolina, 1941

Preserved are portions of England's first New World settlements from 1584 to 1590, and the cultural heritage of American Indians, European Americans, and African Americans who lived on Roanoke Island.

HARPERS FERRY NHP
West Virginia, 1944

This quaint, historic community at the confluence of the Potomac and Shenandoah rivers contains picturesque streets, exhibits, and museums. Hike the trails and battlefields.

LAKE ROOSEVELT NRA
Washington, 1946

Opportunities abound here for boating, fishing, swimming, camping, canoeing, hunting, or visiting historic Fort Spokane and St. Paul's Mission.

CASTLE CLINTON NM
New York, 1946

Located at the southern tip of Manhattan, Castle Clinton served as a defense for New York Harbor, and later a depot through which eight million immigrants entered the United States.

THEODORE ROOSEVELT NP
North Dakota, 1947

The scenic badlands along the Little Missouri River provided a rugged backdrop for the life that TR pursued here and helped shape a conservation policy that we benefit from today.

ADAMS NHP
Massachusetts, 1946

The park preserves and protects the grounds, homes, and personal property of four generations of the Adams family. There is also a library, a church, and a crypt.

91

FORT VANCOUVER NHS
Washington, Oregon, 1948

Explore the lands and structures at the center of fur trade and military history in the Pacific Northwest. Connect to the past and the people who lived and worked here.

FORT SUMTER NM
South Carolina, 1948

Decades of growing strife between North and South erupted in civil war on April 12, 1861, when Confederate artillery opened fire on this Federal fort in Charleston Harbor. Fort Sumter surrendered 34 hours later.

DE SOTO N MEM
Florida, 1948

Commemorating the landing of Spanish explorer Hernando de Soto in 1539, the memorial is comprised of approximately 26 acres on the south shore of the Manatee River.

HAMPTON NHS
Maryland, 1948

In period dress, interpreters guide visitors through the mansion, ice house, and octagon house foundation to tell the story of the enslaved, who made their owners' lavish lifestyle possible.

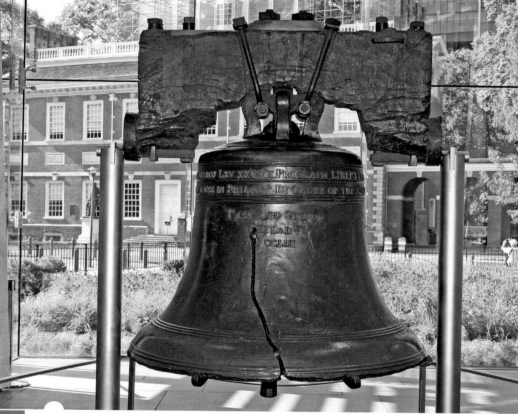

EFFIGY MOUNDS NM
Iowa, 1949

Over 200 American Indian mound sites, ca. 450 BCE to 1300 CE, including 31 effigy mounds in the shapes of birds and bears, are built here to commemorate sacred beliefs.

INDEPENDENCE NHP
Pennsylvania, 1948

Here there are structures and sites associated with the American Revolution and the founding of the United States, including Independence Hall, Congress Hall, Old City Hall, the Liberty Bell, and others.

SAINT CROIX ISLAND IHS
Maine, 1949

The beginning of the French presence in North America began here with an expedition during the winter of 1604-1605. Iced in by freezing temperatures, 35 of 79 men died.

SAN JUAN NHS
Puerto Rico, 1949

The massive masonry fortifications of Castillo San Felipe del Morro, Castillo San Cristobal, most of the city walls, and San Juan Gate, protect this portal to the Americas.

CHRISTIANSTED NHS
Virgin Islands, 1952

The architectural, economic, and political influence of Europe is demonstrated here. The site on the island of St. Croix contains structures from the 1700s and 1800s.

FORT CAROLINE N MEM
Florida, 1950

The climactic battles fought here between the French and Spanish marked the first time that European nations fought for control of lands in what is now the United States.

CORONADO N MEM
Arizona, 1952

Located near the U.S.-Mexican border, the memorial commemorates the first major expedition of Europeans into the American Southwest, led by Francisco Vasquez de Coronado.

GREENBELT PARK
Maryland, 1950

This woodland park features a 174-site campground, nine miles of trails, and three picnic areas to provide many forms of outdoor recreation to visitors year-round.

BOOKER T. WASHINGTON NM
Virginia, 1956

Booker T. Washington was born enslaved on James Burroughs' farm in 1856. His past would influence his philosophies as the most influential African American of his era.

PU'UHONUA O HŌNAUNAU NHP
Hawaii, 1955

A prominent feature is the pu'uhonua (place of refuge) that served as a sanctuary in ancient times for defeated warriors, noncombatants, and those who violated the sacred laws.

FORT UNION NM
New Mexico, 1954

The main unit includes a second fort, a Civil War earthwork, and adobe building ruins of a third fort, built in 1862. A detached unit a mile west encompasses part of the historic grounds of the first Fort Union.

THOMAS EDISON NHP
New Jersey, 1955

The great inventor resided here from 1887 until 1931. The site includes his chemistry lab, machine shop, library, and the world's first motion picture studio.

99

HORSESHOE BEND NMP
Alabama, 1956

Here in 1814, Gen. Andrew Jackson's army attacked the Red Stick Creek warriors. The battle ended the Creek War and created a hero of Andrew Jackson.

PEA RIDGE NMP
Arkansas, 1956

Pea Ridge gets its name from the wild peas that were abundant when whites settled here in the 1820s. The battle and Union victory in 1862 allowed the Union to maintain control of Missouri.

GLEN CANYON NRA
Arizona, Utah, 1958

At over 1.2 million acres, the area includes scenic vistas, geologic wonders, shoreline water-recreation activities, and a huge panorama of human history.

VIRGIN ISLANDS NP
Virgin Islands, 1956

Covering much of the island of St. John, the park is home to early Indian sites, remains of Danish colonial sugar plantations, coral reefs, quiet coves, and sandy beaches.

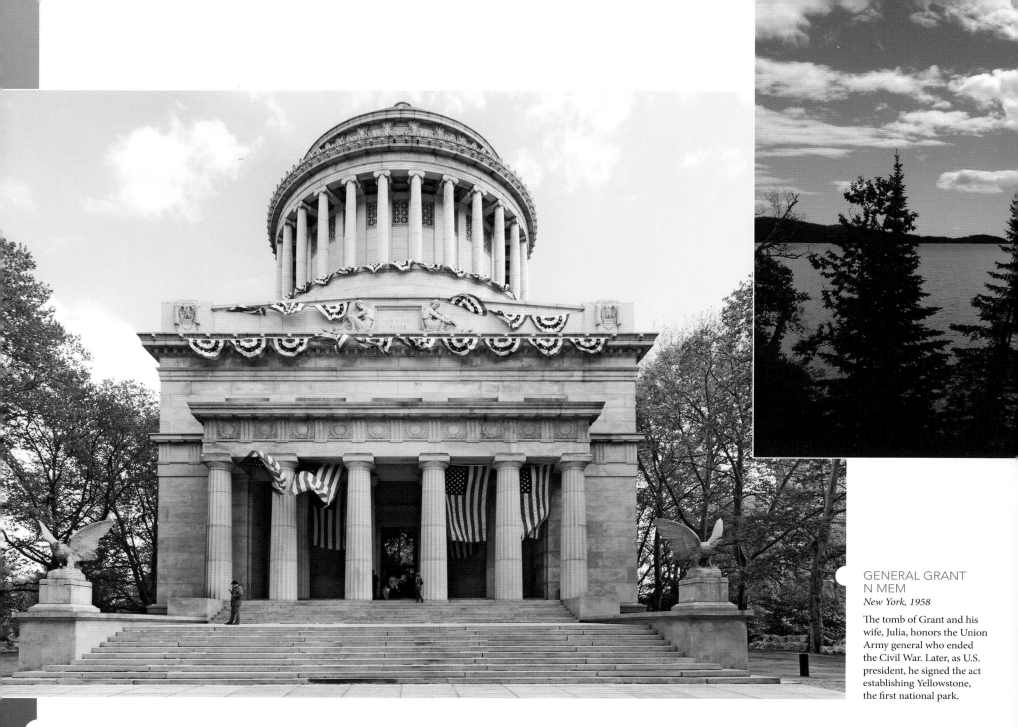

GENERAL GRANT N MEM
New York, 1958

The tomb of Grant and his wife, Julia, honors the Union Army general who ended the Civil War. Later, as U.S. president, he signed the act establishing Yellowstone, the first national park.

LEWIS AND CLARK NHP
Oregon, 1958

This natural setting tells the story of Lewis and Clark's arrival at the Pacific Ocean, winter encampment, exploration, encounters with Indians, and preparation for their return east.

GRAND PORTAGE NM
Minnesota, 1958

This 710-acre monument was established to preserve and interpret fur trade and Ojibwe history and culture. The portage linked one of the main routes for travelers to the Northwest.

MINUTE MAN NHP
Massachusetts, 1959

Visit battlefields, monuments, and structures associated with "the shot heard round the world" that began the Revolutionary War on April 19, 1775.

ARKANSAS POST N MEM
Arkansas, 1960

After the 1803 Louisiana Purchase, the post became part of the United States. By 1819, it was a thriving river port, largest city in the region, and first capital of the Arkansas Territory.

WILSON'S CREEK NB
Missouri, 1960

Fought on August 10, 1861, Wilson's Creek was the first major Civil War battle west of the Mississippi River. Today, it is one of the best-preserved battlefields in the nation.

BENT'S OLD FORT NHS
Colorado, 1960

The fort was an important fur trading post from 1833 to 1849, on the mountain branch of the Santa Fe Trail. It was where traders, trappers, travelers, and Indians met peacefully to trade.

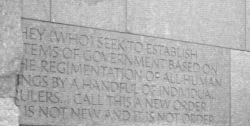

FRANKLIN DELANO ROOSEVELT MEM
Washington, D.C., 1959

The memorial is located along the Cherry Tree Walk on the Tidal Basin near the National Mall. There is a sequence of four outdoor rooms, each reflecting one of FDR's terms in office as president. The memorial was dedicated in 1997.

CAPE COD NS
Massachusetts, 1961

Beaches and bicycle and walking trails offer recreation. Lighthouses, cranberry bogs, and the Marconi Station site—where transatlantic wireless communication was achieved in 1903—provide cultural interest.

RUSSELL CAVE NM
Alabama, 1961

An almost continuous archeological record of human habitation from 10,000 BCE to about 1650 CE is found here. It is named for Thomas Russell, owner of the property when the area was mapped.

FORT DAVIS NHS
Texas, 1961

The fort protected travelers, mail coaches, and freight wagons on the Trans-Pecos portion of the San Antonio-El Paso Road and on the Chihuahua Trail from 1854 to 1891.

FORT SMITH NHS
Arkansas, 1961

One of the first U.S. military posts in the Louisiana Territory, it served to enforce federal Indian policy from 1817 to 1896. There are remains of two frontier military forts and one federal court.

PISCATAWAY PARK
Maryland, 1961

The park provides bird-watching spots, views of Mount Vernon, a place to fish or launch small boats, an 18th-century farm, and a modern-day eco-farm.

HAMILTON GRANGE N MEM
New York, 1962

The home in upper Manhattan was completed in 1802 and named "The Grange." Alexander Hamilton enjoyed his home only until July 11, 1804, when he was fatally wounded in a duel with political rival Aaron Burr.

BUCK ISLAND REEF NM
Virgin Islands, 1961

The finest coral reef gardens in the Caribbean include grottoes, sea fans, and tropical fish, and a snorkel trail provides an opportunity to observe the underwater world.

LINCOLN BOYHOOD N MEM
Indiana, 1962

From 1816 to 1830, Lincoln lived on the southern Indiana farm. Today, it is a working pioneer homestead with a log cabin, outbuildings, split-rail fences, livestock, gardens, and field crops.

THEODORE ROOSEVELT BIRTHPLACE NHS
New York, 1962

Raised in a townhouse at 28 E. 20th St., Roosevelt would become our 26th president. The original brownstone where Roosevelt was born in 1858 was torn down in 1916.

FREDERICK DOUGLASS NHS
Washington, D.C., 1962

Famed abolitionist Frederick Douglass lived here from 1877 to 1895. Born into slavery, Douglass spent his life fighting for justice and equality for all people.

The first human inhabitants were here 5,000 years ago. There are over 120 known village sites within the park, beaches, tall cliffs, lagoons, and offshore bird and sea lion colonies.

SAGAMORE HILL NHS
New York, 1962

Theodore Roosevelt's Queen Anne-style home from 1886 until his death in 1919 was built in 1885 from a plan he sketched. Today, 25 rooms with furnishings that are almost all original are open to the public.

PADRE ISLAND NS
Texas, 1962

The park protects 70 miles of coastline, dunes, prairies, and nesting grounds for sea turtles. It's a haven for 380 bird species, and its rich history includes the Spanish shipwrecks of 1554.

OZARK NSR
Missouri, 1964

The first national park area to protect a river system, it is home to hundreds of freshwater springs, caves, trails, and historic sites.

FORT BOWIE NHS
Arizona, 1964

The fort and Apache Pass were focal points for U.S. military actions against the Chiricahua Apache for control of the region. Adobe walls are left from the posts that stood from 1862 to 1894.

SAINT-GAUDENS NHS
New Hampshire, 1964

Augustus Saint-Gaudens, one of America's greatest sculptors, had his home and studios here. See over 100 of his artworks in the galleries and on the grounds.

JOHNSTOWN FLOOD N MEM
Pennsylvania, 1964

The South Fork Dam failed on Friday, May 31, 1889, and unleashed 20,000,000 tons of water that devastated the town, killing 2,209 people.

FORT LARNED NHS
Kansas, 1964

This well-preserved fort on the Santa Fe Trail was an army post during the Indian Wars era. The troops were known as the Guardians of the Santa Fe Trail.

ALLEGHENY PORTAGE RAILROAD NHS
Pennsylvania, 1964

The first railroad to circumvent the Allegheny Mountains, the portage opened in 1834, creating a direct route between Philadelphia and Pittsburgh.

CANYONLANDS NP
Utah, 1964

Countless canyons and fantastically formed buttes carved by the Colorado River and its tributaries are found here in a primitive desert atmosphere.

FIRE ISLAND NS
New York, 1964

Fire Island preserves ancient maritime forests and historic landmarks and is home to diverse wildlife. The barrier island beaches offer spiritual renewal.

JOHN MUIR NHS
California, 1964

As America's most famous naturalist and conservationist, John Muir fought to protect the wild places he loved, places we can still visit today.

CURECANTI NRA
Colorado, 1965

The reservoirs that make up Curecanti provide amazing water-based recreation high in the Rocky Mountains. Best known for salmon and trout fishing, visitors can also hike, boat, camp, and bird watch.

LAKE MEAD NRA
Nevada, 1964

Lake Mead offers year-round recreational opportunities and is home to thousands of desert plants and animals that have adapted to survive where rain is scarce.

PENNSYLVANIA AVENUE NHS
Washington, D.C., 1965

A street unlike any other, it is known the world over as the heart of the Nation's Capital. America's history has marched, paraded, promenaded, and protested its way along the avenue.

LAKE MEREDITH NRA
Texas, 1965

Through these windswept high plains, the Canadian River has cut dramatic 200-foot canyons, which are a welcoming haven for wildlife and visitors alike.

PECOS NHP
New Mexico, 1965

In the midst of juniper and ponderosa pine woodlands, are the remains of Indian pueblos that stand as meaningful reminders of the people who once prevailed here.

NEZ PERCE NHP
Idaho, 1965

The history and culture of the Nez Perce (Nimiipuu) people is told here. Discover how the Nimiipuu adapted, and today thrive, continuing to make the land their own.

ALIBATES FLINT QUARRIES NM
Texas, 1965

Some 13,000 years ago, this site was used by hunters to get the best stone for their tools. The flint found here was integral for survival, commerce, and culture on the High Plains.

AGATE FOSSIL BEDS NM
Nebraska, 1965

This landscape preserves bones of ancient mammals and reflects many influences, from tribal nations calling it home, to explorers passing through or settling in the American West.

DELAWARE WATER GAP NRA
Pennsylvania, 1965

In this 70,000-acre park, paddlers float down the river, anglers wade the trout streams, and hikers peer into the 1,000-foot-deep Water Gap.

HERBERT HOOVER NHS
Iowa, 1965

Born in a two-room cottage, Herbert Hoover would become president of the United States. The landscape and buildings of his early years reveal how they helped shape the man.

GOLDEN SPIKE NHS
Utah, 1965

On May 10, 1869, the Union and Central Pacific railroads joined their rails at Promontory Summit, completing the first transcontinental railroad.

HUBBELL TRADING POST NHS
Arizona, 1965

Hubell is the oldest operating trading post on the Navajo Nation, selling groceries, grain, hardware, horse tack, coffee, and Native American Art since 1878.

WHISKEYTOWN NRA
California, 1965

This park of 42,000 acres is home to waterfalls, pristine mountain creeks, 70 miles of trails, and opportunities to explore the history of the California Gold Rush.

AMISTAD NRA
Texas, 1965

An oasis in the desert, Amistad is home to a wide variety of plant and animal life and is a great place to camp, hike, and discover its rich cultural history.

ASSATEAGUE ISLAND NS
Maryland, Virginia, 1965

Explore sandy beaches, salt marshes, maritime forests, and coastal bays. Rest, relax, and enjoy some time on the Atlantic coast. Wild horses can also be found at Chincoteague.

ROGER WILLIAMS N MEM
Rhode Island, 1965

Roger Williams was the founder of Rhode Island and a champion of the ideal of religious freedom, allowing those to worship as their conscience dictated.

FORT UNION
TRADING POST NHS
North Dakota, Montana, 1966

Between 1828 and 1867, this was the most important fur trading post on the Upper Missouri River. Northern Plains Indian tribes exchanged buffalo robes for goods from around the world.

CAPE LOOKOUT NS

North Carolina, 1966

Three miles offshore are the barrier islands of Cape Lookout where you can tour historic villages, climb a lighthouse, or go fishing, camping, or birding.

CHAMIZAL N MEM

Texas, 1966

The memorial celebrates the culture of the borderland that helped to peacefully navigate a 100-year border dispute between the United States and Mexico.

GEORGE ROGERS CLARK NHP

Indiana, 1966

Col. George Rogers Clark and his American army captured Fort Sackville from the British on Feb. 25, 1779, assuring the United States' claim to the frontier.

BIGHORN CANYON NRA
Montana, Wyoming, 1966

The vast, wild landscape of over 120,000 acres presents an astounding diversity in ecosystems, wildlife, and over 10,000 years of human history to explore.

SAN JUAN ISLAND NHP
Washington, 1966

This park is known for splendid vistas, saltwater shore, quiet woodlands, orca whales, and one of the last remaining native prairies in the Puget Sound region.

GUADALUPE MOUNTAINS NP
Texas, 1966

This hidden gem is the world's premier example of a fossil reef from the Permian Era and is one of the nation's most pristine wilderness areas.

THEODORE ROOSEVELT INAUGURAL NHS
New York, 1966

Roosevelt took the oath of office as president of the United States on September 14, 1901, here in the Wilcox House after the assassination of President McKinley.

INDIANA DUNES NL
Indiana, 1966

Located on the southern shore of Lake Michigan, the park contains 15,000 acres of rugged dunes, mysterious wetlands, sunny prairies, meandering rivers, and peaceful forests.

WOLF TRAP NP FOR THE PERFORMING ARTS
Virginia, 1966

Located in a setting of rolling hills and woods, the amphitheaters in the park host performances such as musicals, dance, opera, jazz, and popular and country music.

PICTURED ROCKS NL
Michigan, 1966

Sandstone cliffs, beaches, sand dunes, waterfalls, lakes, forest, and 40 miles of shoreline beckon you to visit this park on Lake Superior.

EISENHOWER NHS
Pennsylvania, 1967

This was the home of President Dwight D. Eisenhower. Adjacent to the Gettysburg Battlefield, it served as a weekend retreat and a meeting place for world leaders.

SAUGUS IRON WORKS NHS
Massachusetts, 1968

In the 1600s, iron makers worked in this colony. The site includes working waterwheels, hot forges, mills, and a historic 17th-century home.

SAINT CROIX NSR
Wisconsin, Minnesota, 1968

On this river corridor, you can canoe and camp amid the Northwoods, or boat and fish surrounded by wooded bluffs and historic towns.

JOHN FITZGERALD KENNEDY NHS
Massachusetts, 1967

This is the birthplace and early home of the 35th president. It contains furnishings from the president's childhood and represents the political beginnings of this prominent family.

APPALACHIAN NST
Maine to Georgia, 1968

Completed in 1937, this
2,185-mile-long public footpath
traverses the scenic, wooded,
pastoral, wild, and culturally
resonant lands of the
Appalachian Mountains.

REDWOOD N & SP
California, 1968

Home to the tallest trees on
earth, the park also protects
vast prairies, oak woodlands,
wild riverways, and nearly
40 miles of pristine coastline.

NORTH CASCADES NP
Washington, 1968

Located in the heart of the Cascades, this wilderness park has glaciers, waterfalls, rivers, lakes, lush forests, and a huge diversity of plants and animals.

LAKE CHELAN NRA
Washington, 1968

An alpine landscape beckons here with jagged peaks crowned by glaciers, cascading waters in forested valleys, and communities of life adapting to a changing climate.

FLORISSANT
FOSSIL BEDS NM
Colorado, 1969

Beneath a grassy mountain valley lies one of the most diverse fossil deposits in the world. Petrified redwood stumps and thousands of detailed fossils reveal a prehistoric story.

CARL SANDBURG
HOME NHS
North Carolina, 1968

At this serene place, you can explore the legacy of the man who provided a voice for the American people and who still speaks to us through his words and songs.

BISCAYNE NP
Florida, 1968

Biscayne protects aquamarine waters, emerald islands, and fish-bejeweled coral reefs. Here, too, is evidence of 10,000 years of human history, from pirates to presidents.

ROSS LAKE NRA
Washington, 1968

Ringed by mountains, this area offers an amazing array of outdoor adventures along the Skagit River in the North Cascades.

SLEEPING BEAR DUNES NL
Michigan, 1970

Miles of sand beach, bluffs that tower above Lake Michigan, lush forests, clear inland lakes, and unique flora and fauna make up this picturesque natural world.

LYNDON B. JOHNSON NHP
Texas, 1969

The park presents a unique perspective into the life of our 36th president, from his ancestral history to his final resting place on his beloved LBJ Ranch.

FORD'S THEATRE NHS
Washington, D.C., 1970

President Abraham Lincoln was shot in the theatre on April 14, 1865 while attending a play. He was carried across the street to the Petersen house, where he died the next morning.

WILLIAM HOWARD TAFT NHS
Ohio, 1969

Taft was born and grew up in this two-story Greek Revival house. The environment that shaped Taft's character and philosophy is highlighted on a visit to the site.

ANDERSONVILLE NHS
Georgia, 1970

Andersonville was one of the largest Confederate military prisons during the Civil War. Today, the site is a memorial to all American prisoners of war throughout the nation's history.

FORT POINT NHS
California, 1970

Featuring beautifully arched casemates, Fort Point protected San Francisco harbor from Confederate attack during the Civil War, and from foreign attack after it.

APOSTLE ISLANDS NL
Wisconsin, 1970

Along windswept beaches and cliffs, the 21 islands and 12 miles of mainland shoreline host a blend of cultural and natural resources, including lighthouses that shine their lights over Lake Superior.

VOYAGEURS NP
Minnesota, 1971

Here in the Northwoods, you can immerse yourself in the sights and sounds of a boreal forest, view the dark skies, or travel the interconnected water routes.

141

LINCOLN HOME NHS
Illinois, 1971

Abraham Lincoln resided in this house for 17 years before he became president. The surrounding historic district preserves the 1860s environment in which the Lincoln family lived.

GULF ISLANDS NS
Florida and Mississippi, 1971

Millions of visitors are drawn to the islands in the Gulf of Mexico for the white sandy beaches, aquamarine waters, a boat ride, or to tour an old fort.

BUFFALO NR
Arkansas, 1972

Coursing through massive bluffs, the Buffalo River flows freely for 135 miles and is one of the few remaining undammed rivers in the lower 48 states.

PU'UKOHOLĀ HEIAU NHS
Hawaii, 1972

Ruins of a temple built by King Kamehameha the Great during his rise to power are found here. You can often observe sharks swimming in the bay.

JOHN D. ROCKEFELLER, JR., MEMORIAL PARKWAY
Wyoming, 1972

Linking Yellowstone and Grand Teton national parks, this scenic 82-mile corridor commemorates Rockefeller's role in aiding the establishment of many parks.

GRANT-KOHRS RANCH NHS
Montana, 1972

Once the headquarters of a 10-million-acre cattle empire, Grant-Kohrs Ranch preserves the spirit of the American West and commemorates the role of cattlemen in American history.

LONGFELLOW HOUSE – WASHINGTON'S HEADQUARTERS NHS
Massachusetts. 1972

This was the home of Henry W. Longfellow, one of the world's foremost poets. It also served as headquarters for Gen. George Washington during the Siege of Boston.

FOSSIL BUTTE NM
Wyoming, 1972

Some of the world's best-preserved fossils are found in the flat-topped ridges of this sagebrush desert. They tell a remarkable story of ancient life in a subtropical landscape.

THADDEUS KOSCIUSZKO N MEM
Pennsylvania, 1972

Polish freedom fighter Thaddeus Kosciuszko lived in this house where he received notable visitors such as Chief Little Turtle and Thomas Jefferson.

HOHOKAM PIMA NM
Arizona, 1972

The site is located on the Gila River Indian Reservation and is under tribal ownership. The Gila River Indian Community has decided not to open the area to the public.

CUMBERLAND ISLAND NS
Georgia, 1972

On this barrier island are pristine maritime forests, undeveloped beaches, and wide marshes that whisper the stories of both man and nature.

147

GOLDEN GATE NRA
California, 1972

The park chronicles 200 years of history, from Native American culture to the growth of urban San Francisco, and has splendid opportunities for recreation.

GATEWAY NRA
New York, New Jersey, 1972

Units in Sandy Hook, N.J.; Jamaica Bay and Staten Island, N.Y., combine to make the 26,000 acres of Gateway into one national park.

LYNDON BAINES JOHNSON MEMORIAL GROVE ON THE POTOMAC
Washington, D.C., 1973

President Johnson came here often when he needed to escape from the stresses of the presidency. After he died, his wife chose this place for his memorial.

BIG SOUTH FORK NRRA
Tennessee, Kentucky, 1974

Rich with natural and historic features, the area protects the free-flowing Big South Fork of the Cumberland River and boasts miles of scenic gorges and sandstone bluffs.

149

BOSTON NHP
Massachusetts, 1974

The events and ideas associated with the American Revolution and the founding and growth of the United States provide the common thread linking the sites that compose this park.

CONSTITUTION GARDENS
Washington, D.C., 1974

This 40-acre park was constructed on an island in a lake as a memorial to the 56 Signers of the Declaration of Independence.

BIG THICKET N PRES
Texas, 1974

In this place of discovery, hiking trails and waterways meander through nine different ecosystems, from longleaf pine forests to cypress-lined bayous.

BIG CYPRESS N PRES
Florida, 1974

Protecting over 729,000 acres, these freshwaters contain a mixture of tropical and temperate plant communities that are home to a diversity of wildlife including the Florida panther.

MARTIN VAN BUREN NHS
New York, 1974

Lindenwald was the home of
Van Buren, who served as
U.S. president from 1837-1841.
The grounds and mansion
allow exploration of the nation's
turbulent antebellum period.

CLARA BARTON NHS
Maryland, 1974

This was the headquarters of
the American Red Cross—
founded by Clara Barton—for
seven years. It was her home
for the last 15 years of her life.

KNIFE RIVER INDIAN VILLAGES NHS
North Dakota, 1974

This site was a major Native American trade center for hundreds of years prior to becoming an important marketplace for fur traders after 1750.

SPRINGFIELD ARMORY NHS
Massachusetts, 1974

The world's largest historic U.S. military small arms collection, along with historic archives, buildings, and landscapes are preserved here at the nation's first armory.

JOHN DAY FOSSIL BEDS NM
Oregon, 1974

Colorful rock formations preserve a world-class record of plant and animal evolution, changing climate, and past ecosystems that span over 40 million years.

CUYAHOGA VALLEY NP
Ohio, 1974

A short distance from urban areas, the park is a refuge for native plants and wildlife, with forests, rolling hills, open farmlands, and the winding Cuyahoga River.

TUSKEGEE INSTITUTE NHS
Alabama, 1974

Booker T. Washington recruited the best and the brightest to teach here. Innovations in agriculture expanded Tuskegee's standing throughout the country.

CANAVERAL NS
Florida, 1975

Many threatened animals find protection on this barrier island, including sea turtles that nest on its pristine shores. Indians and early settlers fished the lagoons.

NINETY SIX NHS
South Carolina, 1976

Here, settlers struggled to survive, Cherokee Indians fought to keep their land, and two Revolutionary War battles that claimed over 100 lives took place.

OBED WSR
Tennessee, 1976

In the late 1700s, the river was a fishing and hunting area for trappers and pioneers. Today, the Obed offers visitors a variety of outdoor recreational opportunities.

VALLEY FORGE NHP
Pennsylvania, 1976

Site of the 1777-1778 winter encampment of the Continental Army, the park honors the sacrifices of the Revolutionary War soldiers and civilians.

KLONDIKE GOLD RUSH NHP
Alaska, Washington, 1976

In 1897, word of a rich gold strike in northwestern Canada ignited dreams of easy riches. The story of the stampede to the Yukon goldfields and Seattle's role in this event are told here.

EUGENE O'NEILL NHS
California, 1976

America's only Nobel Prize-winning playwright, Eugene O'Neill, made his home here at the height of his writing career. He wrote his final and most memorable plays here.

LOWELL NHP
Massachusetts, 1978

Lowell's water-powered textile mills catapulted the nation—including immigrants and female factory workers—into a new industrial era. Lowell is a living monument to the Industrial Revolution.

ELEANOR ROOSEVELT NHS
New York, 1977

The only national historic site dedicated to a first lady, Eleanor Roosevelt named this modest house Val-Kill. She would come here as a retreat from her busy life.

CONGAREE NP
South Carolina, 1976

Astonishing biodiversity and the largest intact expanse of old-growth bottomland hardwood forest remaining in the southeastern United States exist here.

FORT SCOTT NHS
Kansas, 1978

The site's structures, parade ground, and tallgrass prairie, bear witness to the era when the country was forged from a young republic into a united transcontinental nation.

CHATTAHOOCHEE RIVER NRA
Georgia, 1978

Along this river valley, you can enjoy nature's display, raft leisurely through the rocky shoals, fish the misty waters as the sun rises, and picnic on a warm afternoon.

PALO ALTO BATTLEFIELD NHP
Texas, 1978

On May 8, 1846, U.S. and Mexican troops clashed on the prairie of Palo Alto. The causes, events, and consequences of the U.S.-Mexican War are examined here.

WAR IN THE PACIFIC NHP
Guam, 1978

The former battlefields serve as a reminder of the World War II battles fought here, while the verdant jungles, sandy beaches, and turquoise waters beckon visitors.

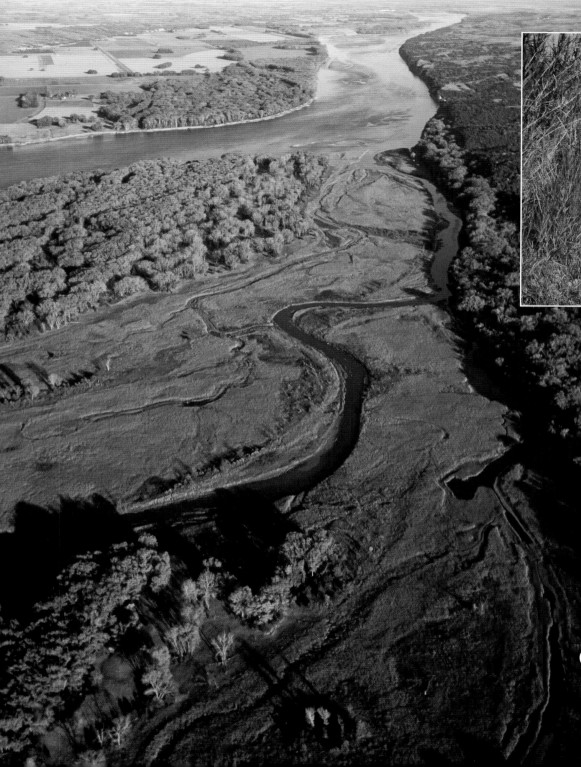

RIO GRANDE WSR
Texas, 1978

Spirited adventure can be found on this river flowing between limestone cliffs, which, along with the wetland corridor, is the lifeblood of the desert.

SAN ANTONIO MISSIONS NHP
Texas, 1978

Four Spanish frontier missions, part of a colonization system that stretched across the Southwest in the 1600s, 1700s, and 1800s, are preserved here.

MISSOURI NRR
South Dakota, Nebraska, 1978

Two free-flowing stretches of the Missouri, North America's longest river, make up this park. Enjoy the untamed and mighty river that flows as nature intended.

EDGAR ALLAN POE NHS
Pennsylvania, 1978

Poe wrote some of his most popular tales here in Philadelphia. In this humble home, one may reflect on his astonishing creativity.

MIDDLE DELAWARE NSR
Pennsylvania, 1978

The largest free-flowing river in the eastern United States, the Delaware River runs past forests, farmlands, and villages.

NEW RIVER GORGE NR
West Virginia, 1978

A rugged, whitewater river flowing northward through deep canyons, the New River is among the oldest rivers on the continent. The park encompasses over 70,000 acres of land.

FRIENDSHIP HILL NHS
Pennsylvania, 1978

Albert Gallatin was secretary of the treasury during the Jefferson and Madison administrations. Friendship Hill is his restored country estate.

MAGGIE L. WALKER NHS
Virginia, 1978

Maggie Walker devoted her life to civil rights advancement. Her home is preserved as a tribute to her enduring legacy of vision, courage, and determination.

SAINT PAUL'S CHURCH NHS
New York, 1978

Saint Paul's Church helps to tell the story of the development of colonial society and the road to the American Revolution. The 18th-century church was used as a Revolutionary War hospital.

EBEY'S LANDING NH RES
Washington, 1978

This stunning landscape at Puget Sound's gateway preserves historical, agricultural, and cultural native and Euro-American traditions and offers spectacular opportunities for recreation.

UPPER DELAWARE SRR
Pennsylvania, New York 1978

Canoe through rapids and quiet pools. Fish in one of the northeastern United States' finest fishing rivers. The clean water supports a healthy ecosystem and offers tranquility and excitement.

THOMAS STONE NHS
Maryland, 1978

Living a planter's and lawyer's comfortable life until war with Great Britain loomed, Stone risked everything to safeguard American rights and became one of the signers of the Declaration of Independence.

KALOKO-HONOKŌHAU NHP
Hawaii, 1978

To survive, native Hawaiians used ancient fishing skills, built fishponds, and learned how to find fresh water. The people's spirit and knowledge of the elders created a tradition of respect and reverence for this area.

ANIAKCHAK NM & PRES
Alaska, 1978

Its remote location and challenging weather make this one of the park system's most wild and least-visited places. It is home to a deep caldera formed during a massive volcanic eruption 3,500 years ago.

SANTA MONICA MOUNTAINS NRA
California, 1978

The mountains offer easy access to surprisingly wild places, Malibu's famous beaches, or over 500 miles of trails. Historical and cultural sites abound, from old movie ranches to American Indian centers.

BERING LAND BRIDGE N PRES
Alaska, 1978

Explore a wilderness dotted with hot springs, ancient lava flows, and the world's largest maar lakes. The land bridge provided a way for plants, animals, and people to cross from old world to new.

YUKON-CHARLEY RIVERS N PRES
Alaska, 1978

Located in Interior Alaska, the site offers exploration in a largely untouched landscape. Geology, cultural history, gold rush remnants, and vast scenery are part of the experience.

KOBUK VALLEY NP
Alaska, 1978

Caribou, sand dunes, the Kobuk River, and Onion Portage are just some of the park's features. Half a million caribou migrate through the valley. The Kobuk River is an ancient pathway for people and wildlife.

GATES OF THE ARCTIC NP & PRES
Alaska, 1978

This vast landscape has no roads or trails. Discover intact ecosystems where people have lived with the land for thousands of years. It remains virtually unchanged except by the forces of nature.

CAPE KRUSENSTERN NM
Alaska, 1978

The monument forms 70 miles of shoreline on the Chukchi Sea. Over 114 beach ridges provide evidence of human use for 5,000 years, and the Inupiat continue to use the area today.

KENAI FJORDS NP
Alaska, 1978

Here, the ice age lingers. Wildlife thrives in the icy waters and forests. Native Alutiiq relied on these resources, but today, shrinking glaciers bear witness to the effects of our changing climate.

NOATAK N PRES
Alaska, 1978

The Noatak River environs feature some of the Arctic's finest arrays of plants and animals. The river is classified as a national wild and scenic river and offers stunning wilderness float-trip opportunities.

WRANGELL-ST. ELIAS NP & PRES
Alaska, 1978

Within this wild landscape, people have been living off the land for centuries and still do today. The park is a rugged yet inviting place to experience your own adventure.

LAKE CLARK NP & PRES
Alaska, 1978

Here is a land of great beauty, where volcanoes steam, salmon run, bears forage, craggy mountains reflect in shimmering turquoise lakes, and local people still depend on the land and water.

WORLD WAR II VALOR IN THE PACIFIC NM
Hawaii, Alaska, California, 1980

Here, the stories of the Pacific War, including the events at Pearl Harbor, internment of Japanese Americans, battles in the Aleutians, and occupation of Japan are preserved and interpreted.

FREDERICK LAW OLMSTED NHS
Massachusetts, 1979

Recognized as the founder of American landscape architecture and the nation's foremost park maker, Olmsted established the world's first full-scale professional office for the practice of landscape design.

BOSTON AFRICAN AMERICAN NHS
Massachusetts, 1980

Centered on the north slope of Beacon Hill, the African American community of 19th-century Boston led the city and the nation in the fight against slavery and injustice.

VIETNAM VETERANS MEMORIAL
Washington, D.C., 1980

Honoring the men and women who served in the Vietnam War, the memorial chronologically lists the names
of over 58,000 Americans who gave their lives in service to their country. The memorial was dedicated in 1982.

JAMES A. GARFIELD NHS
Ohio, 1980

In 1880, Garfield used his front porch as a platform to greet thousands of well-wishers during his presidential campaign. Today, the porch serves as a gateway to the story of the Garfield family.

ALAGNAK WR
Alaska, 1980

The Alagnak River traverses the beautiful Alaska Peninsula, providing an unparalleled opportunity to experience the unique wilderness, wildlife, and cultural heritage of southwest Alaska.

MARTIN LUTHER KING, JR., NHS
Georgia, 1980

Visit MLK's birth home and where he played as a child. Walk in his footsteps, hear his voice in the church where he moved hearts and minds. Marvel at how he was an instrument for social change.

POTOMAC HERITAGE NST
Maryland, Washington, D.C.,
Virginia, Pennsylvania, 1983

The trail network follows paths explored
by George Washington. You can follow
the same routes today—on foot,
bicycle, horse, or by boat.

KALAUPAPA NHP
Hawaii, 1980

Since 1866, over 8,000 people have died
at Kalaupapa. Kalaupapa is refuge for the
few remaining residents now cured of
Hansen's disease (leprosy) but forced to
live their lives in isolation.

NATCHEZ TRACE NST
Mississippi, 1983

The 450-mile foot trail was the lifeline
through the Old Southwest. Experience
portions of that journey on foot the way
earlier travelers did. Today, there are five
separate trails totaling over 60 miles.

WOMEN'S RIGHTS NHP
New York, 1980

The park tells the story of the first Women's Rights Convention held in Seneca Falls in July 1848. It is a story of struggles for civil rights, human rights, and equality—global struggles that continue today.

KOREAN WAR VETERANS MEMORIAL
Washington, D.C., 1986

Our nation honors her sons and daughters who answered the call to defend a country many never knew and a people most never met. The memorial was dedicated in 1995.

HARRY S TRUMAN NHS
Missouri, 1983

Visitors can experience the surroundings Truman knew as a young man of modest ambition, through his political career, and final years as a former president.

STEAMTOWN NHS
Pennsylvania, 1986

Here you can learn the history of steam railroad transportation and the people who built, repaired, and rode during this special era in America's industrial history.

JIMMY CARTER NHS
Georgia, 1987

The rural southern culture that revolves around farming, church, and school had a large influence in molding the character and shaping the political policies of the 39th U.S. president.

183

TIMUCUAN E & H PRES
Florida, 1988

One of the last unspoiled coastal wetlands
on the Atlantic Coast includes 6,000 years
of human history, salt marshes, coastal
dunes, hardwood hammocks, Fort Caroline,
and Kingsley Plantation.

EL MALPAIS NM
New Mexico, 1987

Volcanic forces over the past million years have created cinder cones, shield volcanoes, collapses, trenches, caves, and other eerie formations that preserve continuous geologic records of volcanism.

SAN FRANCISCO MARITIME NHP
California, 1988

Stand on the stern of *Balclutha*; feel the fresh wind blowing in from the ocean. Adjacent to Fisherman's Wharf, the park offers the sights, sounds, smells, and stories of Pacific Coast maritime history.

185

CHARLES PINCKNEY NHS
South Carolina, 1988

This coastal-plantation remnant preserves the story of Charles Pinckney, his life of public service, the lives of enslaved African Americans on Lowcountry plantations, and their influences on him.

POVERTY POINT NM
Louisiana, 1988

At its peak 3,000 years ago, Poverty Point was part of a trading network that stretched for hundreds of miles. Explore the culture of a sophisticated people who left behind an important archeological site.

CITY OF ROCKS N RES
Idaho, 1988

Emigrants from the California Trail described the rocks as "a city of tall spires," "steeple rocks," and "the silent city." Today, the reserve attracts rock climbers, campers, hikers, hunters, and the adventurous.

NATIONAL PARK OF AMERICAN SAMOA
American Samoa, 1988

The park invites you into a world of sights, sounds, and experiences like no other in the United States.
Enjoy the welcoming people of American Samoa, its rich culture and natural resources.

NATCHEZ NHP
Mississippi, 1988

The magnificent antebellum estate, Melrose, represents the height of Southern prosperity. The William Johnson House tells of the life of free African Americans in the pre-Civil War South.

MISSISSIPPI NRRA
Minnesota, 1988

In the middle of a bustling urban setting, this 72-mile river park offers quiet stretches for fishing, boating, and canoeing. Other spots are excellent for bird watching, bicycling, and hiking.

HAGERMAN FOSSIL BEDS NM
Idaho, 1988

The collection contains over 200 different species of fossil plants and animals: saber-toothed cat, mastodon, bear, camel, ground sloth, and more. Over 3,000 new fossil fragments are found each year.

BLUESTONE NSR
West Virginia, 1988

The river and the rugged, ancient gorge it has carved is a diverse and scenic area of the Southern Appalachians. It provides a living landscape and a haven for a variety of plants and animals.

189

PETROGLYPH NM
New Mexico, 1990

One of the largest petroglyph sites
in North America, it features designs
and symbols carved onto volcanic
rocks by American Indians and
Spanish settlers 400 to 700 years ago.

ULYSSES S. GRANT NHS
Missouri, 1989

The Civil War general who saved the Union
and became 18th president of the United States
lived here with his wife, Julia Dent, and her
family at her family home, White Haven,
from 1854 to 1859.

WEIR FARM NHS
Connecticut, 1990

The Weirs transformed their summer retreat into a creative refuge for friends and fellow artists. After Weir, artists Mahonri Young and Sperry Andrews also lived and worked here, continuing Weir's legacy.

GAULEY RIVER NRA
West Virginia, 1988

The 25 miles of free-flowing Gauley River and the six miles of the Meadow River pass through scenic gorges and valleys containing a wide variety of natural and cultural features.

MARY MCLEOD BETHUNE COUNCIL HOUSE NHS
Washington, D.C., 1991

The Council House was the first headquarters of the National Council of Negro Women and Mary McLeod Bethune's last home in Washington, D.C.

慰霊塔

MANZANAR NHS
California, 1992

Manzanar War Relocation Center was one of 10 camps where Japanese American citizens and resident Japanese aliens were interned during World War II.

SALT RIVER BAY NHP & E PRES
Virgin Islands, 1992

A blend of sea and land includes some of the largest remaining mangrove forests in the Virgin Islands, coral reefs, and a submarine canyon.

NIOBRARA NSR
Nebraska, 1991

High water quality and the relatively free-flowing nature of the Niobrara River support diverse life, and unique fossil-filled sandstone cliffs are home to over 200 waterfalls.

MARSH-BILLINGS-ROCKEFELLER NHP
Vermont, 1992

The park is a living symbol of three generations of conservationist thought and practice and a repository for the histories of three quintessentially American families.

LITTLE RIVER CANYON N PRES
Alabama, 1992

Natural resources and cultural heritage come together to tell the story of the preserve, a special place in the Southern Appalachians.

DAYTON AVIATION HERITAGE NHP
Ohio, 1992

Three exceptional men, Wilbur Wright, Orville Wright, and poet Paul Laurence Dunbar, found their creative outlet here and offered the world hope and the ability to make a dream a reality.

BROWN V. BOARD OF EDUCATION NHS
Kansas, 1992

This site commemorates the 1954 U.S. Supreme Court decision that ended racial segregation in public schools. Its story is one of hope and courage.

GREAT EGG HARBOR NSRR
New Jersey, 1992

This 129-mile river gradually widens as it picks up the waters of 17 tributaries on its way to Great Egg Harbor and the Atlantic Ocean.

MOJAVE N PRES
California, 1994

Singing sand dunes, volcanic cinder cones, Joshua tree forests, and carpets of wildflowers are all found at this 1.6 million-acre park that provides serenity and solitude.

KEWEENAW NHP
Michigan, 1992

From 7,000 years ago to the 1900s, people mined Keweenaw copper. Native peoples made copper into tools. In the 1800s, investors and immigrants developed industries and communities here.

DRY TORTUGAS NP
Florida, 1992

The park is known for the magnificent Fort Jefferson, picturesque blue waters, superlative coral reefs and marine life, and a vast assortment of bird life.

CANE RIVER CREOLE NHP
Louisiana, 1994

The nearly 300-year relationship between the Cane River Creoles and their homeland was shaped by the river. The Creole culture endures and thrives to this day.

NEW ORLEANS JAZZ NHP
Louisiana, 1994

Only in New Orleans could there be a national park for jazz! A variety of musicians here explore the origins, development, and progression of New Orleans jazz.

WASHITA BATTLEFIELD NHS
Oklahoma, 1996

This is the setting along the Washita River where Custer led his troops on a surprise attack against a Southern Cheyenne village on November 27, 1868.

NICODEMUS NHS
Kansas, 1996

Nicodemus, the oldest remaining black settlement west of the Mississippi, represents the involvement of African Americans in the westward expansion and settlement of the Great Plains.

LITTLE ROCK CENTRAL HIGH SCHOOL NHS
Arkansas, 1998

Little Rock Central High School is recognized for the role it played in the desegregation of public schools in the United States.

NEW BEDFORD WHALING NHP
Massachusetts, 1996

In the mid-19th century, New Bedford was the whaling capital of the world. Whaling made New Bedford a cosmopolitan seaport community and one of the richest cities in the world.

BOSTON HARBOR ISLANDS NRA
Massachusetts, 1996

Tour a Civil War-era fort, visit historic lighthouses, explore tide pools, hike, camp, fish, picnic, and swim—all within reach of downtown Boston.

TALLGRASS PRAIRIE N PRES
Kansas, 1996

The preserve protects a nationally significant remnant of the once vast tallgrass prairie and its cultural resources. Here, the tallgrass prairie takes its last stand.

MINUTEMAN MISSILE NHS
South Dakota, 1999

This site tells the story of Minuteman Missiles, nuclear deterrence, and the Cold War—one of the most important eras in the history of America and the world.

TUSKEGEE AIRMEN NHS
Alabama, 1998

The first African American military pilots began their flight training at Moton Field in Tuskegee, Alabama. This site tells their story.

ROSIE THE RIVETER/ WORLD WAR II HOME FRONT NHP
California, 2000

Through historic structures, museum collections, interpretive exhibits, and programs, the park tells the diverse and fascinating story of the WWII home front.

FIRST LADIES NHS
Ohio, 2000

The home of First Lady Ida Saxton McKinley and the seven-story 1895 City Bank Building are preserved at this site, which honors our nation's first ladies.

VIRGIN ISLANDS CORAL REEF NM
Virgin Islands, 2001

This tropical marine ecosystem includes mangroves, sea grass beds, coral reefs, and extraordinary blue-green waters as well as a habitat for humpback whales, sea turtles, and reef fish.

FLIGHT 93 N MEM
Pennsylvania, 2002

The memorial honors the courageous action of 33 passengers and seven crew members on Flight 93 who thwarted a possible attack on our Nation's Capital.

MINIDOKA NHS
Idaho, 2001

The history and cultural resources associated with the relocation and internment of thousands of Japanese Americans during WWII are interpreted here.

GOVERNORS ISLAND NM
New York, 2001

The island is a vibrant summer seasonal venue of art, culture, and performance
against the backdrop of two centuries of military heritage and New York City skyline.

CEDAR CREEK AND BELLE GROVE NHP
Virginia, 2002

Site of the Battle of Cedar Creek, October 19, 1864, this park also contains Belle Grove Plantation, home of an early Shenandoah settler.

AFRICAN BURIAL GROUND NM
New York, 2006

The African Burial Ground dating from the 17th century was rediscovered in 1991 during the construction of a federal office building. It is now a place of honor.

WORLD WAR II MEMORIAL
Washington, D.C., 2004

Through architecture and sculptures, the World War II Memorial recognizes the Americans who served, honors those who fell, and pays tribute to the victory they achieved to restore freedom.

PRESIDENT WILLIAM JEFFERSON CLINTON BIRTHPLACE HOME NHS
Arkansas, 2010

Bill Clinton spent his first formative years in Hope, Arkansas, where he learned many of the early lessons that defined his life and his presidency.

SAND CREEK MASSACRE NHS
Colorado, 2007

On November 29, 1864, U.S. soldiers attacked a peaceful encampment of Cheyenne and Arapaho along Sand Creek. This site enhances public understanding of that tragedy.

CARTER G. WOODSON HOME NHS
Washington, D.C., 2006

Dr. Woodson's home served as the headquarters for the Association for the Study of African American Life and History. In 1926, he established what today is Black History Month. The home is in need of restoration and is closed to the public.

PORT CHICAGO NAVAL MAGAZINE N MEM
California, 2009

On July 17, 1944, at Port Chicago Naval Magazine, 320 men were instantly killed when two ships being loaded with ammunition for the Pacific theater troops exploded.

RIVER RAISIN NBP
Michigan, 2010

The park preserves, commemorates, and interprets the January 1813 battles of the War of 1812 that resulted in victory for American Indians and defeat for the United States.

FORT MONROE NM
Virginia, 2011

The monument spans American history: American Indian presence, Captain John Smith's journeys, a haven for Civil War freedom seekers, and a defense for the Chesapeake Bay.

CÉSAR E. CHÁVEZ NM
California, 2012

The most important Latino leader in the United States during the 20th century, Chávez led farm workers in the establishment of the country's first permanent agricultural union.

MARTIN LUTHER KING, JR. MEMORIAL
Washington, D.C., 2011

Captured in a moment of reflective thought, the figure of civil rights leader Martin Luther King, Jr., serves as the forward element of the Stone of Hope.

PATERSON
GREAT FALLS NHP
New Jersey, 2011

Paterson, America's first planned industrial city, centered around the Great Falls of the Passaic River. From humble mills would rise industries that changed the face of the nation.

CHARLES YOUNG
BUFFALO SOLDIERS NM
Ohio, 2013

In spite of overt racism and stifling inequality, Young rose through the military ranks to become one of the most respected leaders of his time.

HARRIET TUBMAN
UNDERGROUND
RAILROAD NHP
Maryland, 2013

Harriet Tubman was the Underground Railroad's best-known conductor who risked her life to guide nearly 70 enslaved people to new lives of freedom in the North.

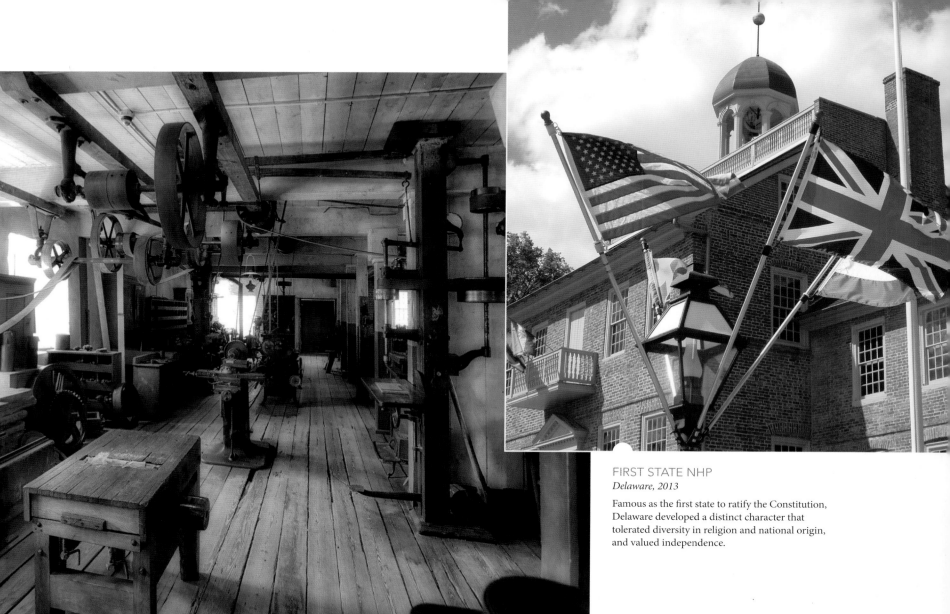

FIRST STATE NHP
Delaware, 2013

Famous as the first state to ratify the Constitution, Delaware developed a distinct character that tolerated diversity in religion and national origin, and valued independence.

BLACKSTONE RIVER VALLEY NHP
Massachusetts, Rhode Island, 2014

The elements that turned this quiet valley into an industrial powerhouse are still present today, including the river, canal, mill villages, and an agricultural landscape.

The preserve features a supervolcano, elk, historic cabins, and prehistoric sites at the southern edge of the Rocky Mountains. Camping, hiking, fishing, and horseback riding await visitors.

TULE SPRINGS FOSSIL BEDS NM
Nevada, 2014

Mammoths, lions, and camels once roamed along wetlands just north of what is now Las Vegas, Nevada. Their history is preserved here.

PULLMAN NM
Illinois, 2015

Designed as a utopia, Pullman was a place to provide workers with a safe community and better standard of living, free of social ills.

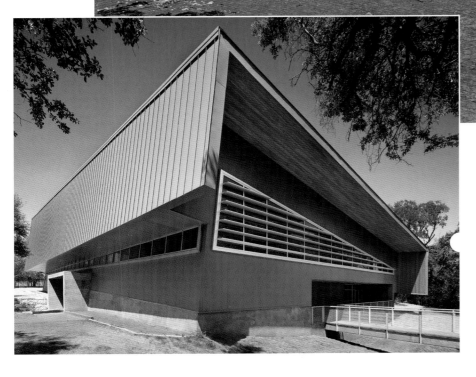

HONOULIULI NM
Hawaii, 2015

The monument tells the history of internment and martial law in Hawaii during World War II. It is a place to reflect on wartime experiences and recommit ourselves to freedom and justice.

WACO MAMMOTH NM
Waco, Texas, 2015

This paleontological site preserves the nation's only recorded discovery of a nursery herd of Columbian mammoths. View fossils including female mammoths, a bull mammoth, and a camel that lived approximately 67,000 years ago.

Photo Credits

Page 8: left-Greg Gnesios, right-William Sunderland; 9: top-Denice Swanke, bottom-John D. Giorgis; 10: top-Gavin Emmons, bottom-NPS; 11: l-Sharon A. Murray, r-Carol Highsmith; 12: l top-Amanda L. Smith, r-NPS, bottom-Sharon A. Murray; 13: Buddy Secor; 14: l-John D. Giorgis, r-Barbara Vietzke; 15: top-Steven Redman, bottom-Ingrid Sensor; 16: l top-NPS, r top-Vidur K. Sharma, bottom-Dale L. Pate; 17: Barbara Vietzke; 18: l-Yvonne Manske, r-Barbara Vietzke; 19: Michael B. Chutz; 20: l-Brian Bailey, r-Kevin Sweeney; 21: Davis Stevenson; 22: l-Gizella Betak, r-Gavin Emmons; 23: Alice Kong; 24: l-Ken Kraushaar, r-John D. Giorgis; 25: l-Karen Hughes, r-Tim Hauf; 26: l-NPS, r-Harold Jerrell; 27: l-Barbara Vietzke, r-Katy Kildee, bottom-David Schneider; 28: l-NPS/Stephanie Martin, r-Greg Gnesios; 29: l-Yvonne Manske, r-Dale Pate; 30: l-NPS, r-Kevin Bacher; 31: l-Barbara Vietzke, r-Cindy McIntyre; 32: l-Jennifer Applebaum, r-Barbara Vietzke; 33: top-Stacy Humphreys, bottom-Gavin Gardner; 34: Kathy Carbonetti; 35: NPS; 36: l-NPS/Janice Wei, r-Norma Thrower; 37: Cindy McIntyre; 38: l-Nancy Stewart, r-Harold Jerrell; 39: l-Barbara Vietzke, r-Brian Bailey; 40: top-NPS, bottom-Robert Jensen; 41: l-James Emert, r-NPS/Matthew Thomas; 42: l-Richard Maxwell, r-NPS/Tom Engberg; 43: l-NPS, r-NPS/Andrew Kuhn; 44: Barbara Vietzke; 46: l-Suzanne Moody, r-Dave Clark; 47: NPS/Peter Jones; 48: l-NPS, r-John Donoghue; 49: l-John Cipriani, r-Joel Cadoff; 50: l top-James Emert, r top-Marjorie Fairweather, bottom-Tim Ervin; 51: inset-Barbara Vietzke; 52: top-Jesse Barden, bottom-NPS; 53: NPS/Neal Lewis; 54: l-Jackie Wheet, r-Douglas Prouty; 55: l-Jim B. Lewis, r-Hank Schmoyer, bottom-Afton Woodward; 56: top-Gavin Gardner, l-Sharon A. Murray, r-NPS, bottom-Sharon A. Murray; 57: Harold Jerrell; 58: inset top-James Emert, inset bottom-Ellen Martin, r-Steven Miller; 59: inset-Kyle Ackerman; 60: l-NPS, r-NPS; 61: top-NPS, bottom-David Woolridge; 62: top-Chuck Wagner, bottom-Ana Pratt; 63: l-Jennifer Applebaum, r-NPS; 64: top-NPS, bottom-Lisa Lynch; 65: l-Barbara Vietzke; 66: top-Daniel Beards, bottom-Drew Jackson; 67: Steven Milller; 68: Carol Highsmith; 69: l-John D. Giorgis, r and bottom-Carol Highsmith; 70: top-Sharman Ayoub, bottom-Glenn Gardner; 71: Sonya Smith; 72: l top-NPS, l bottom-Rick Kendall, r-Harold Jerrell; 73: Carol Highsmith; 74: l-Kendra Hinkle, r-Harold Jerrell; 75: l-Kent Bolke, r-Jefferson National Parks Association; 76: John Hazard; 77: all NPS; 78: l-John D. Giorgis, r-NPS; 79: top-Bill Little, bottom-Kevin Bacher; 80: top-Norma Thrower, bottom-Ingrid Sensor; 81: l-NPS/Dave Krueger, r-NPS; 82: top-Tim Hauf, bottom-NPS; 83: l top-Peter Santos, r-NPS/Terry Wildy, bottom-Michael Evans; 84: l-Steve Dean, r-Dakota McCoy; 85: both NPS; 86: Harold Jerrell; 87: top-Kevin Daley, center-NPS/William Urbin, bottom-Joseph M. Phillips; 88: top-NPS, center r-Randall Becker, center l-Rick Kendall, bottom-Rob Bolling; 89: NPS/Mark Muse; 90: Vidur K. Sharma; 91: l-NPS, r-Quang-Tuan Luong, bottom-Elizabeth Brown; 92: l-NPS, r-Brent Everitt; 93: top-NPS, bottom-Rick Kendall; 94: l-Daniel Beards, r top-NPS, r bottom- Jessica Dumas; 95: NPS; 96: l-NPS, r top-David Goldstein, r bottom-NPS; 97: Laura Fawcett; 98: Bill Tucker; 99: l top and bottom-NPS, r-Afton Woodward; 100: l-Steve Black, r-NPS, bottom-NPS/B. Moffitt; 101: NPS; 102: l-Kevin Daley, r-Cathy Nagle-Ervin; 103: top-NPS, bottom-Lou Sideris; 104: l-Jeremy Smith, r-Charles Dischinger; 105: top-NPS, bottom-Daniel Beards; 106: l-Mary Dawson, r-Barbara Vietzke; 107: top-Max Kandler, bottom-Pat Schmidt; 108: l-David Goldstein, r-John D. Giorgis; 109: top-Kevin Daley, bottom-NPS; 110: top-Kevin Daley, bottom-NPS; 111: l-NPS, r-Brian Bailey; 112: top-NPS, bottom-NPS/Chuck Bloomingburg; 113: Suzanne Moody; 114: top-Kevin Daley, bottom-Chuck Wagner, r-Doug Kuony; 115: inset-NPS;

116: Steven Miller; 117: top-Luther Bailey, bottom-Stephen von Hagen; 118: top-NPS/Lisa Lynch, center-Gavin Gardner, bottom-Carol Highsmith; 119: Andrew Cattoir; 120: l-NPS/Suze Havener, r-NPS/Eric Valencia; 121: top-Gavin Gardner, bottom-Lil Mansfield; 122: l-Nicholas Homyak, r-Dale L. Pate; 123: top-NPS, bottom-Gavin Gardner; 124: top-Mark Edward Fox, center-Greg Garetz, bottom-John K. Robson; 125: Barbara Vietzke; 126: l-Emily Sunblade, r-NPS; 127: l-Brian McCutchen, r-Lily Aguilar; 128: Randall Rakes; 129: l-Jonathan Welde, r-Gary Tarleton; 130: l-Jeff Manuszak, r-Lenora Henson; 131: l-Nathan Adams, r-Chris Case; 132: top-NPS/Katie Lawhon, bottom-Kevin Turausky, r-NPS/Jean Van Tatenhove; 133: inset-Sara Patton; 134: l-Greg Walter, r-Jon Parmentier; 135: top-NPS, bottom-Keith Brumand-Smith; 136: l-NPS, inset-NPS, r-NPS; 137: inset-Shauna Cotrell; 138: D. Arthur Brown; 139: top-Cynthia Dorminey, l-John Donoghue, r-NPS; 140: l-NPS/Kirke Wrench, r-Christopher Barr; 141: top-Neil Howk, bottom-NPS; 142: l-NPS, r-Dave Mull; 143: Gail Bishop; 144: top-Richard Maxwell, l-Debra Crow, r-William Ognibene; 145: NPS/Phil Petersen; 146: Cindy McIntyre, inset-Gavin Gardner; 147: NPS; 148: top-Marc Solomon, bottom-Dan Krebs; 149: Miriam Matthias, inset-Carol Highsmith; 150: top-Daniel Beards, bottom-Carol Highsmith; 151: l-Wynn Carney, r-Michael Black; 152: both NPS; 153: l-James Langone, r-NPS; 154: l-NPS/Scott Ritner, r-NPS; 155: l-NPS/Sue Simenc, r-Cindy Lewis; 156: NPS; 157: l-Jeff Oates, r top-Rusty Wilson, r bottom-Richard Aroksaar; 158: l-Higgins & Ross, r top-NPS/Luther Bailey, r bottom-Rick Kendall; 159: NPS; 160: inset-Reed Hartford, r-Morning Washburn; 161: top-Richard Maxwell, bottom-Mya Cooper; 162: l-Greg Latza, r-Brian Bailey; 163: l-Afton Woodward, r-Hank Schmoyer; 164: l-NPS, r top-NPS, r bottom-John Donoghue; 165: Leah Perkowski-Sisk; 166: r-Kevin Daley, l-Steven Redman, bottom-NPS/Alan Hageman; 167: Hank Schmoyer; 168: Lawrence Goldman; 169: l-Brian Bailey, r-NPS/Roy Wood; 170: l-Arianne Lindholm, r-NPS/Josh Spice; 171: NPS/Katie Cullen; 172: Paxton Woelber; 173: l-Rebecca Talbott, r-Paul Stolen; 174: MK MacNaughton; 175: l-John D. Giorgis, r-Alaska ShoreZone; 176: l-Mona McKindley, r top-Donny Chambers, bottom-Sentidra Joseph; 177: Suzanna Sigona; 178: l-NPS, r-NPS/Brett Nigus; 179: inset-NPS; 180: l-Matt Page, r-NPS; 181: l-NPS/Emily Davie, r-NPS; 182: Matthew Turner; 183: l-Ron Rothberg, r-Afton Woodward, bottom-Hugh Peacock; 184: Will Dickey; 185: l-NPS/Dale L. Pate, inset-NPS; 186: l-Wallace Keck, r top-Brent Everitt, r bottom-Louisiana Office of Tourism; 187: NPS/Michael Larson; 188: l-NPS, inset-Gordon Dietzman, r-NPS; 189: inset-NPS/David Bieri; 190: l-Howard Holley, r-David Newmann; 191: l-Xiomaro, r-NPS/Gary Hartley; 192: l-NPS/Kenneth Chandler, r-Brian Bailey; 193: both NPS; 194: top-Ed Sharron, l and r-NPS; 195: NPS/Gail Bishop; 196: l-Brian Bailey, r-NPS/Wild and Scenic Rivers, r bottom-Dan Johnson; 197: Shauna Cotrell; 198: l-NPS/Dusty Fuqua, r-Liz Dupree; 199: l-Brian Bailey, r-NPS; 200: all NPS; 201: Gavin Gardner; 202: both NPS; 203: l-Luther Bailey, r-NPS; 204: r top-Chuck Wagner, l-NPS, r-Brian Bailey; 205: Daniel Krebs; 206: Carol Highsmith; 207: l-Hank Schmoyer, r-Kevin Daley; 208: l-Christian H. Davis, r-NPS/Mario Medina; 209: l-Brian Bailey, r-NPS, bottom-Daniel D. Downing; 210: Carol Highsmith; 211: l-U.S. Army, r-Ruben Andrade; 212: Daniel Krebs; 213: r-NPS/Tom Engberg, l-NPS; 214: l-NPS, r-Russ Smith; 215: Rob Dixon; 216: both NPS; 217: l-Waco Parks Dept; r-NPS.

IHS – International Historic Site
N & SP – National and State Parks
NB – National Battlefield
NBP – National Battlefield Park
NBS – National Battlefield Site
NHP – National Historical Park
NHP & PRES – National Historical Park and Preserve
NH RES – National Historical Reserve
NHS – National Historic Site
NL – National Lakeshore
NM – National Monument
NM & PRES – National Monument and Preserve
NMP – National Military Park
N MEM – National Memorial
NP – National Park
NP & PRES – National Park and Preserve
N PRES – National Preserve
NR – National River
NRA – National Recreation Area
NRR – National Recreational River
NRRA – National River and Recreation Area
N RES – National Reserve
NS – National Seashore
NSR – National Scenic River/Riverway
NST – National Scenic Trail
PKWY – Parkway
SRR – Scenic and Recreational River
WR - Wild River
WSR – Wild and Scenic River

Cover photograph – Colorado NM by Donna Fullerton. Backcover l-r: Acadia NP by Kent Miller, Independence NHP by Daniel Beards, Grand Teton NP by Harold Jerrell, Fredericksburg and Spotsylvania County Battlefields NMP by Buddy Secor, Thomas Jefferson MEM by Carol M. Highsmith. Page 5 – Theodore Roosevelt NP by Quang-Tuan Luong, Page 6 – Acadia NP by Barbara Vietzke.

Design by Kathy Carbonetti

The National Park Service website and the National Parks Index were used as source materials for the parks' text. Thanks to all NPS personnel who contributed to these sites.

For more information about our national parks, visit www.nps.gov